# REPAIRING OLD
## AND
## HISTORIC WINDOWS

# REPAIRING OLD AND HISTORIC

# WINDOWS

## A MANUAL FOR ARCHITECTS AND HOMEOWNERS
## NEW YORK LANDMARKS CONSERVANCY

**The Preservation Press**
National Trust for Historic Preservation

66849

The Preservation Press
National Trust for Historic Preservation
1785 Massachusetts Avenue, N.W.
Washington, D.C. 20036

The National Trust for Historic Preservation is the only private, nonprofit organization chartered by Congress to encourage public participation in the preservation of sites, buildings, and objects significant in American history and culture. Support is provided by membership dues, endowment funds, contributions, and grants from federal agencies, including the U.S. Department of the Interior, under provisions of the National Historic Preservation Act of 1966. The opinions expressed here do not necessarily reflect the views or policies of the Interior Department. For information about membership in the National Trust, write to the Membership Office at the address above.

This book was initially prepared by the Ehrenkrantz Group, Architects and Planners, for the New York Landmarks Conservancy and edited by Wesley Haynes, Harry Hansen, and Mark A. Weber. Richard Pieper wrote all captions for the photographs and illustrations.

Printed in the United States of America
96 95 94 93 92   5 4 3 2 1

Library of Congress Cataloging in Publication Data

Repairing old and historic windows / New York Landmarks
Conservancy.
       p.    cm.
    Includes bibliographical references (p. ) and index.
    ISBN 0-89133-185-9
    1. Windows—Maintenance and repair. 2. Historic build-
    ings—Maintenance and repair. 3. Historic buildings—
    Conservation and restoration. I. New York Landmarks
    Conservancy.
    TH2275.R47 1992                    91-15622
    694.6—dc20

Designed and typeset by J. Scott Knudsen, Park City, Utah
Printed by Thomson-Shore, Dexter, Michigan
Cover: Repairing a window in the Evening Star building,
Washington, D.C. (Photo courtesy Carol Highsmith)

# CONTENTS

Acknowledgments                                                    7

Introduction                                                       9

1  WINDOWS IN AMERICAN ARCHITECTURE:                              15
   A HISTORICAL OVERVIEW, 1620–1950

2  EVALUATING WINDOW CONDITIONS AND PROBLEMS                       49

3  MAINTAINING, REPAIRING, AND RETROFITTING WINDOWS                97

4  REPLACING WINDOWS                                              133

5  REHABILITATING WINDOWS IN LANDMARK BUILDINGS                   153

REHABILITATION STANDARDS AND GUIDELINES                           161

Notes                                                             165

Glossary                                                          169

Information Sources                                               191

Further Reading                                                   193

Index                                                             197

# ACKNOWLEDGMENTS

The subject of window replacement in landmark buildings is no less controversial today than it was eight years ago when the New York Landmarks Conservancy commissioned a study on the subject. A concern for energy efficiency and the legacy of the oil crisis of the mid-1970s, as well as local tax incentives offered through New York's J-51 program, led many owners of architecturally distinguished buildings then being rehabilitated to scrap perfectly serviceable windows for new ones. All preservationists applauded the drive to extend the useful life of these buildings through rehabilitation, but what was being saved? In many cases the replacement of original windows drastically altered a building's appearance and historical character.

The Conservancy responded to this dilemma with a series of questions. How do old windows compare to today's replacement windows with respect to quality of construction, physical performance, and maintenance? Can old windows be upgraded to meet contemporary performance standards? Can new windows be redesigned to resemble traditional designs? These and subsequent questions formed the core of the Conservancy study, conducted in 1985, and the study became the basis for this manual.

The study identified the most prevalent window types in buildings now being restored and compiled information on the current range of available products for window rehabilitation in historic buildings. Approximately 150 manufacturers producing a range of window products were polled and asked for information describing their products. Also requested and submitted were energy test data and specific examples of the use of the products in historic buildings.

The materials submitted by manufacturers and installers were subsequently analyzed to determine the impact and results of the various strategies and products. The study's primary goal was to provide the tools for making responsible decisions. A secondary goal was to indicate areas where further developments in the industry and expanded product lines are needed.

The study was made possible through generous public and private financial support. Grants were awarded from the Design Arts Program of the National Endowment for the Arts and the Solar Cities Program of the Department of Energy as well as from the National Trust for Historic Preservation, J. M. Kaplan Fund, New York State Council on the Arts, DeVac Corporation, Marvin Lumber and Cedar Company, Pittsburgh Plate Glass Industries Foundation, Schlegel Corporation, and Silverstein Properties.

The data compiled by the study were transformed into a research report by the Ehrenkrantz Group, Architects and Planners, under the direction of the Technical Preservation Services Center of the New York Landmarks Conservancy. The staff of the Ehrenkrantz Group who contributed to the report were Ezra Ehrenkrantz, FAIA, principal; Theodore H. M. Prudon, associate principal; Kate Burns Ottavino, historic preservation specialist; Suzanne Smith, energy analyst; Linda Fiske, administrative assistant; Mark Segalla, consultant; and Susan Swiatosz, consultant.

Another source of information was S. Robert Hastings and W. Richard Crenshaw's "Window Design: Design Strategies to Conserve Energy," a title in the series of publications *NBS Building Science Series 104*, from the National Bureau of Standards (U.S. Department of Commerce). The glossary was taken in part from the Schlegal Corporation's catalog and in part from the glossary in *Speaking of Windows*, a publication of the Small Homes Council–Building Research Council connected with the University of Illinois, Urbana-Champaign.

The Conservancy is grateful to the following individuals, who lent their diverse technical expertise while serving as advisers to the study: Jan C. K. Anderson, RESTORE; Barry Donaldson, AIA, Tishman Research Corporation; Andrew Forgatch, Window Systems; Frank Hetman, DeVac Corporation; Marilyn Kaplan, New York State Office of Parks, Recreation, and Historic Preservation; John P. Loguidice, JPL International; Adam F. Ramez, Silverstein Properties; Frank Sanchis, then at the New York City Landmarks Preservation Commission and now with the National Trust for Historic Preservation; John Stoller, Schlegel Corporation; Morris Taylor, Marvin Lumber and Cedar Company; Mark Ten Eyck; and Joyce Underberg, Schlegel Corporation.

The staff of the New York Landmarks Conservancy who contributed to this project included Susan Henshaw Jones, executive director; Laurie Beckelman, former executive director; Carol Clark and Wesley Haynes, former project directors; and Mark A. Weber, project director; Kevin Murphy and Diane Cohen, former project managers; and Stacey Mink and Anita Rask, administrative assistants.

The Conservancy also wishes to thank The Preservation Press of the National Trust for Historic Preservation for agreeing to publish the project's findings and thereby disseminating this important information to a larger audience.

# INTRODUCTION

The purpose of this book is to provide a better understanding of the problems and potential of windows in old buildings. It also offers advice on diagnosis and rehabilitation measures within accepted preservation standards, that is, the 10 standards promulgated by the National Park Service of the U.S. Department of the Interior as the Secretary of the Interior's Standards for Rehabilitation (see page 161).

Anyone considering spending thousands of dollars to replace windows should find the information here helpful. Today's replacement window market is largely uncharted territory. The vast array of replacement windows available readily leads to confusion about which one, if any, is best for a particular situation.

But is replacement really necessary? The authors dispute the claim that the only good window is a new window. Repairing and maintaining an essentially sound window is often a far more sensible approach. Besides retaining the character of the interior and exterior, the existing window may actually be superior to its replacement with respect to materials, details, and construction. Also, when retrofitted with weatherseals, additional glazing, draperies, and shutters, it may have the potential to meet contemporary energy and acoustic characteristics expected of replacement windows.

This guide to window repair will help in analyzing windows, objectively assessing their condition, and tackling problems that affect the residents' or workers' health and comfort while maintaining the building's value.

No one wants to spend much time concentrating on a building's condition, but the fact remains: all windows, new or old, require regular maintenance. Otherwise, they rapidly deteriorate and can damage adjacent parts of the building; in addition, their energy efficiency declines drastically. With fuel costs uncertain, replacement windows may be seen as a means of immediately reducing energy consumption.

If the windows rattle and leak, repair is urgently needed. Often windows appear to be in worse condition than they actually are. In many cases painting, scraping, and adjustments to stops and weatherstrips are inexpensive approaches to making loose windows tight.

If replacement is the best strategy, the owner should be aware of various options. While costs vary, replacement windows can become a big expenditure. Even when working within a limited budget, settling for an inexpensive replacement window can prove a false economy: the added cost of maintaining the less-expensive new window will increase its original cost many times over (unless, of course, maintenance needs are deliberately ignored, and the window is simply replaced again within a decade).

In the past two decades the restoration and rehabilitation of existing buildings has become an increasingly larger part of the construction industry's workload. Old buildings are no longer demolished and replaced with impunity but are more often recycled as a means of providing new, valuable space at a reasonable cost. Thus, old buildings and all their original components, including windows, are of concern not only to owners but also to architects, engineers, preservation consultants, and builders.

The collaborative experience of design professionals, the window industry, and preservation agencies has yielded replicable strategies in rehabilitating windows within preservation guidelines. In addition, the development of new products and procedures, unavailable a decade ago, has expanded the range of options, making it easier to save an old window than replace it.

Rehabilitating an essentially sound building and restoring it to a usable condition eliminates not only the cost of demolition but also the time and costs associated with constructing a new building. The value of the rehabilitated building, both architectural and financial, will ultimately depend on not only its appearance and condition but also how well it meets its programmatic requirements. Thus, the savings achieved from retaining the basic building structure may be applied to the careful restoration of the building's historic character to make it more competitive for sale or rental.

Windows are a problem in nearly every rehabilitation project. Typically they are likely to be visibly deteriorated because of the lack of routine maintenance, such as painting and caulking. When further considerations of energy efficiency and noise prevention are weighed and lead time in ordering new parts is estimated, an owner may initially conclude that replacement windows are a necessity.

But there are good reasons to give the existing windows a second thought and a closer look. To begin with, recycling the existing windows may fully meet the project's requirements less expensively and with the added benefit of preserving irreplaceable original design elements of the building. For example, many species of wood used in constructing windows before World War II are more durable than species available today. In addition, the elegant thin sections used in making early 20th-century steel casements now are extremely difficult to replicate.

A closer look at existing windows is also required when approvals are sought from preservation agencies for replacing windows in buildings designated as landmarks or being considered for federal rehabilitation tax credits. These agencies encourage retaining the original windows when possible but permit replacement if the need is substantiated by a detailed survey of conditions. The proposed replacement windows also must meet rigorous design criteria.

No one solution is best for every case. Every project presents new opportunities. This manual encourages following a systematic approach when deciding whether or not to replace windows. It makes a case for rehabilitating existing windows when possible and practical but replacing them when necessary. As such, perhaps it will shed objective light on a controversial subject.

The authors define window rehabilitation as the process of returning a window to a state of utility and improving its performance to contemporary standards. Rehabilitation includes repair, retrofit, and replacement.

Windows are rehabilitated for many reasons, but the authors have assumed three common underlying objectives: to improve the window's energy efficiency, to minimize the cost to maintain it, and to restore the visual character of the building. With these objectives in mind, the first step is to determine the windows' architectural significance. The first chapter gives an overview of the historical development of windows in the eastern United States.

The next step is to inspect the existing windows, noting their condition and how well they operate, and to assess their potential for rehabilitation. Problems of a general nature or peculiar to a specific window type can then be identified and the scope of the rehabilitation effort outlined. The second chapter presents problems likely to be encountered in old windows. These problem areas include physical condition, energy efficiency, and maintenance-related issues. Once the windows' condition is assessed and specific problem areas are identified, the appropriate treatments may be investigated and the scope of work outlined and determined. The chapter concludes with descriptions of the conditions that warrant using either repair or replacement approaches.

The third step is determining a rehabilitation strategy to meet the project's goals within a budget. The nonreplacement strategies—maintenance, repair, and retrofit—are outlined in the third chapter. Information on replacement windows is presented in chapter four.

Preparing a manual discussing every type of window in the United States would have been a limitless undertaking. The American window evolved on a regional basis to meet local climatic conditions within the limits of local building traditions. But certain commonalities among windows exist across the country.

Thus, while the scope of examples here is limited primarily to those in the Northeast, the rehabilitation strategies, methods, and evaluations presented are suitable to buildings located in all areas of the country. The buildings discussed are architecturally and historically significant and are eligible to be or already are designated as landmarks. They, therefore, serve as excellent models of rehabilitation. Also included are specific concerns of windows of buildings in urban areas, such as noise infiltration and wind load.

For owners of designated landmarks or those seeking a tax credit for the certified rehabilitation of a historic structure, chapter five provides insight on what aspects of windows will be considered significant by review agencies. The Secretary of the Interior's Standards for Rehabilitation, a useful set of standards for any project involving restoring or repairing an old building, follow this chapter.

# REPAIRING OLD
# AND
# HISTORIC WINDOWS

# 1

# Windows in American Architecture: A Historical Overview, 1620–1950

The technological and stylistic development of the window in American architecture is itself a subject worthy of a book. Because of the sheer quantity of window types and the number of regional variations, this chapter attempts to provide only an overview of the subject. The goal is to help owners and design professionals place in a broader context the windows in a specific building or surrounding buildings. The authors have attempted to identify certain features associated with the construction and appearance of windows in various building types from different periods, but the information should not be applied too literally. Not all buildings rigorously adhere to stylistic dictates, and local tradition often supersedes.

At any given time in history building components are constructed and used within certain technological limits. A description of American window construction techniques, which lagged behind that of Europe until the late 19th century, is presented first and followed by a chronological description of how windows were used and what they looked like in residential, public, commercial, and industrial buildings.

In isolating the window from the rest of the building the authors have drawn on standard field guides to American architecture for general dates for architectural style.[1] Some of the research collected in preparing this material was previously published.[2] Many terms used in this overview are defined in the glossary.

## GLASS MAKING

Glass manufacturing markedly influenced window design. The size, shape, and other visual characteristics of the glass pane established

Opposite: Six-light, double-hung sash add texture and scale to the facade of this early 19th-century residence in New York State's Catskill Mountains. (Richard Pieper)

**Blowing and swinging cylinder glass.**

**Spinning glass in a "flashing furnace" to make a crown-glass disk.**

the design parameters of windows before the Civil War. When rehabilitating early American windows, the condition, texture, and color of the glass are especially important.

Early glass in America was made by two distinct methods—the cylinder glass method and the crown glass method. Cylinder glass, also called broad or sheet glass, provided larger sheets of glass of uniform thickness, but it was more brittle than well-made crown glass. The latter provided material of higher quality with fewer inherent imperfections.

The cylinder glass method required several steps. A large cylinder of glass was blown on a blow pipe and scored; when cooled, the ends were removed, and the cylinder was slit lengthwise. Subsequently the cylinder was reheated and opened to form a flat sheet. Generally the cylinders were 8 or 10 inches in diameter and some 24 to 30 inches in length. Some changes were later made in the process, and by the 19th century blowing and the additional process of swinging allowed much larger cylinders to be made—up to 16 to 18 inches in diameter and even 7 feet in length.

In the crown glass method, a bubble formed on a blow pipe was opened at the bottom. By continuously enlarging the opening and twirling the glass, a more or less flat disk, called a table, was produced. The tables usually ranged in size from 3 to 5 feet in diameter. While this method resulted in waste, a high-quality glass could be obtained. Rectangular panes of glass were cut from the disk; the bump remaining in the center where the pipe had been attached, called the bull's eye, was typically used in places, such as transoms, where transparency was not as important. The bull's eye was rarely used in a prominent

16

part of the window in the 17th and 18th centuries, although it is often an exaggerated feature of 20th-century revival styles or "art" windows.

Early crown and cylinder glass can be recognized today by their imperfections and color. Small air bubbles were common in each. Crown glass often contains concentric ripples, whereas parallel marks are common in cylinder glass. Also common in these older glass types is a blue-green, yellow, or reddish tint. The blue-green cast results from small amounts of iron oxides present in most sands used to make glass. To eliminate this tinting, early glass makers added manganese, which reacts to ultraviolet light over time by turning pinkish and sometimes yellow.

The availability and manufacturing of window glass had a direct impact on the configuration and development of window sash. By the 1620s window glass was apparently available in this country as a result of English imports, although earlier attempts had been made to manufacture glass domestically. The more durable crown glass was better suited to transportation, and window panes were costly, small, and few in number. The first use of glass was generally in diamond-shaped panes set in lead cames. It was not until the end of the 17th century that square panes became available.

Until the beginning of the 19th century, American-made glass was a limited product. European-made glass was easily available in shipping centers, where it was distributed upon importation. Technological developments in American glass making followed those on the Continent.

At the beginning of the 18th century the Georgian style was introduced, and the medieval-type casement window, often with a fixed top light, was replaced with the more "modern" vertical sliding sash window. These double-hung sash windows, commonly equipped with multiple panes measuring 6 by 8, 7 by 9, 8 by 10, 9 by 11, and 10 by 12 inches, became the window type of choice. By the beginning of the 19th century the sizes had again increased, and multiple panes of 8 by 10, 9 by 11, 10 by 12, and 10 by 14 inches were available. Glass was occasionally manufactured domestically, but English and continental imports were the main source of supply well into the 19th century.

As a domestic cylinder glass industry emerged, glass panes became even larger, less expensive, and more readily available, and sash became proportionately larger. In the 18th century double-hung sash windows with eight-over-twelve, twelve-over-twelve, and nine-over-nine lights were common. By the end of the century six-over-six lights was the most common configuration. Simultaneously, the shape of the panes themselves changed. Early sash generally have almost square panes, which by the end of the 18th century changed to a larger sheet of a more vertical character.

In the 19th century other specialized architectural glass-making processes were developed. Pressed glass provided diversity in patterns and textures. Curved shapes were formed by using bent glass. More

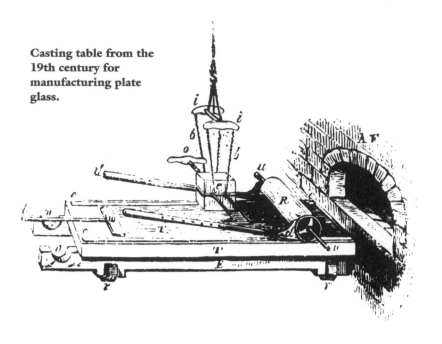

Casting table from the 19th century for manufacturing plate glass.

Daniel Badger's 1865 design for a sidewalk vault makes innovative use of cast glass.

common, however, was stained and colored glass. Its use was revived in the 1830s, and by midcentury it had again achieved a major acceptance in religious architecture. On a smaller scale the use of leaded and multicolored glass was common in residential and commercial buildings during the second half of the 19th century.

A more important method of manufacturing glass was the plate glass process, first developed in Great Britain at St. Helens in 1773.

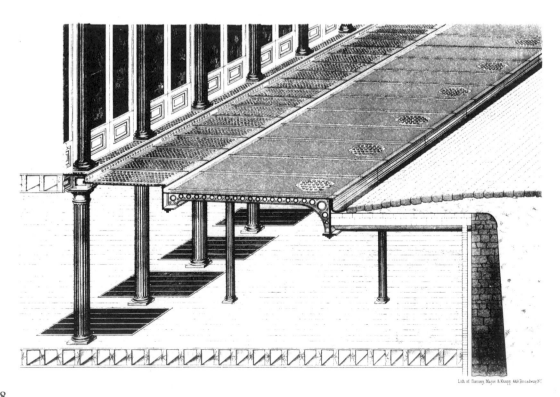

Lith. of Sarony, Major & Knapp, 449 Broadway, N.Y.

More affordable plate glass was not available until 1832, when the continental cylinder process was improved by using a larger cylinder and cutting it with a diamond cutter. Because it was cast in larger sheets on a casting table with a uniform surface, plate glass had less distortion than cylinder glass and thus was more attractive for use in storefronts.

By the late 1830s imported plate glass was available in this country, and by the midcentury very large sheets were available. By then, attempts were also being made to manufacture plate glass domestically. The improvement in quality, increase in size, and availability of larger sheets of plate glass led to the use of one-over-one windows by the end of the Civil War. The production of domestic plate glass in the 19th century increased steadily, although English and other imports were widely used.

The invention of sidewalk lights as "vault lights," patented in 1845 to allow natural light to reach basement storage areas, utilized cast-glass disks fixed into iron gratings strong enough to support pedestrian traffic. By the 1870s glass blocks were inserted in floors and floor slabs.

Wire glass was another important development in the 19th century. Steel sash glazed with wire glass was an early attempt to fireproof windows, and wire glass became known as "fireglass." By the turn of the century wire glass came in various patterns with such names as

**Vault lights, developed in the 19th century, have glass disks set in cast-iron frames that illuminate areas below steps and sidewalks. (Richard Pieper)**

19

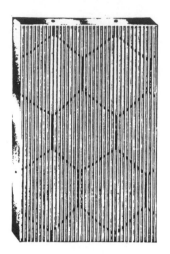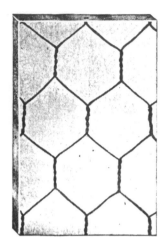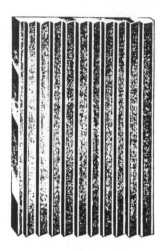

**Patterns of wire glass.**

Ondoyant Glass. The Pittsburgh Hardwood Door Company's catalog of 1911, for example, pointed out reduced insurance costs for buildings equipped with this glass, and it is commonly found today in windows located in fire stairs or in building walls adjacent to other buildings, where wire glass is used in "lot-line windows."

Glass manufacturing diversified during the 20th century. The process of making plate glass improved while remaining essentially unchanged, and the processes of manufacturing float glass and drawn glass were developed. Cumulatively, these advances made possible the emergence of the glass curtain wall, ultimately transforming the walls of the largest skyscraper into single windows. In the drawn glass process the glass was passed through rollers, much like the contemporary plate glass process, in which molten glass flows through rollers. Rolled or roughcast glass is made in a similar manner and can be patterned by modifying the face of the rollers. A more recent development is float glass, in which glass is rolled onto water.

"The history of architecture," wrote the French architect Le Corbusier, "is the history of the struggle for the window."[3] The benchmarks of this evolution are clear when tracing the development of architectural glass making. Nonetheless, it would be inaccurate to conclude that this technological revolution determined the design of windows in all cases. As early as the 1880s many window designers returned to the use of smaller glass panes, even in large windows, strictly for stylistic effect. The survival of the multipaned window, used primarily in residential buildings today, attests to this fact.

## WOODWORKING AND JOINERY

Wood windows are more difficult to date on the basis of their joinery and details because traditional methods of woodworking persisted for long periods of time. Before the 1840s nearly all American wood

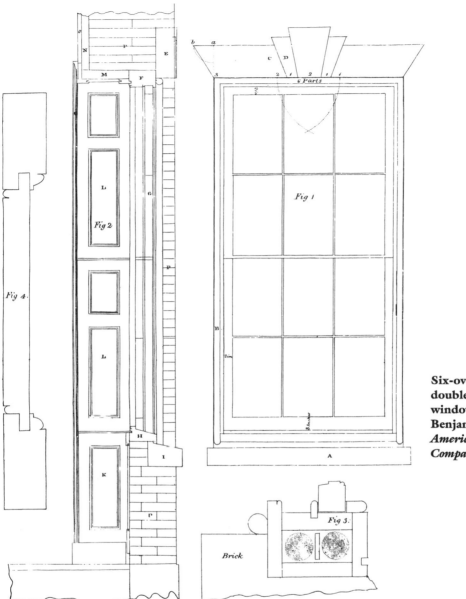

**Six-over-six, double-hung window. (Asher-Benjamin's *The American Builder's Companion*, 1806)**

windows were constructed exclusively by hand tools that were relatively primitive compared to the saws, chisels, and planes available today. Nonetheless, many surviving wood windows from this period exhibit superb craftsmanship in their close joinery and elegantly attenuated muntins. Power-driven saws and molding machinery capable of cutting and shaping finish work gradually were introduced into window production before the Civil War, particularly in trim, but most sash continued to be fabricated primarily by hand until late in the century.

A study of window construction between 1810 and 1868 in Schermerhorn Row, New York City, was made in preparation for the

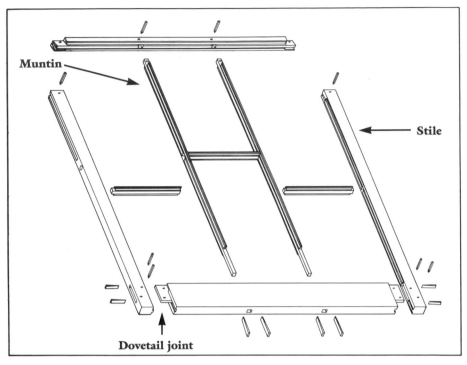

Early 19th-century, double-hung sash construction: meeting rails join stiles with a dovetail joint, and vertical muntins pass through the lower rail. (Michael J. Devonshire)

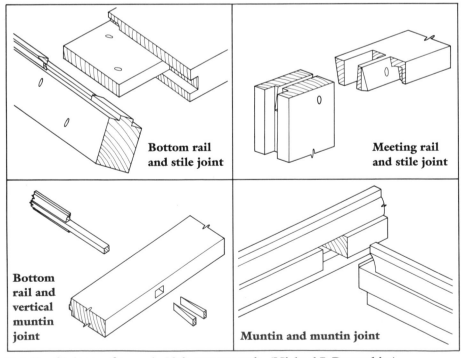

Details of joinery of an early 19th-century sash. (Michael J. Devonshire)

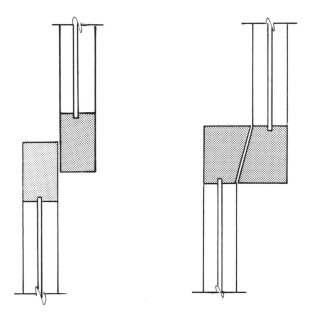

**Plain and beveled meeting rails. (Anne T. Sullivan)**

restoration of the block in 1981 and is the most thorough analysis of 19th-century window technology in the city to date.[4] The six-over-six, double-hung sash and frames dating from the period of original construction (1810–12) were constructed similarly to a window published in Asher Benjamin's *The American Builder's Companion* of 1806, with a boxed frame consisting of butt-jointed boards and a countersunk parting stop. Sash from this period were 1¼ inches and were joined with mortise-and-tenon joints pegged and wedged with wood at the corners. The meeting rail was connected to the stiles with a shallow dovetail joint, and the ends of the muntins were tenons extending continuously through the sash rails.

Although the joinery was virtually identical, sash from the 1840s were constructed of 1¹¹⁄₁₆-inch stock. Six-over-six sash installed in 1868 to match existing sash reveal a different method of joinery. Muntin tenons were not continuous through the rails, metal pins replaced the wooden pegs and wedges at the corner joints, and the meeting rail was connected to the stiles with a bridle joint formed by a slot mortise-and-tenon. How typical these developments were is yet to be fully assessed, but the joinery of the 1868 window was typical of sash construction through the end of the century. All mortise-and-tenon joints were eventually cut more precisely by machine.

Meeting rails were flush (plain rail) or beveled (check or lip rail) as early as 1800, although the latter indicated a more expensive window. Plain rail sash, typically held open with pegs or spring bolts, were available for replacement in the late 19th century, but check rail sash were more common in new construction before the end of the century.

## METAL WORKING

Metal was first used in windows for hardware and glazing bars. Wrought iron was used for hinges, latches, and handles. Early sash occasionally used wrought iron or lead for glazing bars. Metal hardware to counterbalance windows was imported as early as 1800.

The standardization of window production in the late 19th century led to the development of new patented cast- or extruded metal hardware to make windows easier to operate and more energy efficient. Counterbalancing windows, consisting of chain or cord pulleys and lead, bronze, or cast-iron sash weights, were available through catalogs.

As early as the 1870s large commercial and industrial windows were sometimes carried in iron frames, but not until the turn of the century did recent improvements in the process of hot rolling steel result in the widespread use of steel windows.

## WINDOWS IN RESIDENTIAL BUILDINGS

The size, proportion, and style of windows play a major role in a building's appearance. In many ways the historical development of windows in the eastern United States from the beginning of the 19th century reflects a growing cognizance by architects and builders of the diverse possibilities in window design.

Seventeenth-century American windows, introduced by European settlers, were plain; only a few survive today. Glass, which was scarce and costly, was used sparingly, and many early windows contained

**Traditional Dutch windows have fixed upper sash and lower inward-swinging casements separated by a heavy horizontal mullion. (Anne T. Sullivan)**

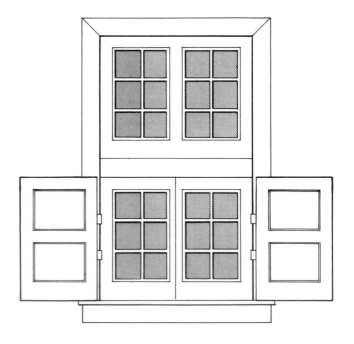

only small, stationary sash. Wood or iron casement sash commonly followed English building practice. Most of these early stationary and casement sash had diamond-shaped glass panes set in lead cames and reinforced by iron bars. Fenestration was not necessarily symmetrically arranged during this period.

Early windows that survive in buildings following Dutch construction practice were different. These windows often consisted of leaded upper and lower sections, separated by a heavy horizontal bar. The upper section was stationary and located in the front, toward the outside of the frame, while the lower section was set in a casement placed toward the inside of the frame, hinged to swing inward. The exterior of the casement was protected by outswinging shutters placed in front of the window frame.

By the early 18th century stationary and casement sash began to be replaced by vertical sliding or double-hung sash. This new sash type appears to have achieved popular acceptance between 1720 and 1735. Double-hung sash were easily adapted to existing or enlarged window openings and found widespread application. Early double-hung or enlarged sash contained no cord, pulley, or sash weights, and only the lower sash was operable. This sash was fixed, either closed in place or open in several positions with a wood peg inserted into holes. This window type remained common throughout the 18th century and well into the 19th century, especially in vernacular structures. More substantial windows used double- or even triple-hung sliding sash.

**Jethro Coffin House, Nantucket, Massachusetts, c. 1686. Early wood casement sash were often mounted in pairs in a single window opening. Sash met at a center dividing mullion, as shown here, or at lapped interlocking rabbets on the stiles of opposing sash. (Mark A. Weber)**

25

Early vertical sliding sash gained acceptance by about 1735. Upper sash frequently were fixed, with lower sash supported when open with pegs set into holes in the jambs. Note wide wood muntins. (Karen Patteson)

The stylistic detailing of this window type as well as the number of lights or panes per sash changed over time. Usually symmetrically arranged, windows of the Georgian (c. 1700–1800) and Federal (c. 1780–1820) periods contained operating sash and were elegantly detailed; thin muntins and mullions conveyed an overall impression of light and air. Early Federal-style row houses typically had small-paned, six-over-six windows. This development was closely related to the development of glass-manufacturing technology.

The Georgian and Federal periods also included designs for special window types. Front entrances, for example, would often be emphasized by a semicircular window with fixed, leaded transoms. Arched window heads often appeared in gable ends with the muntins and mullions arranged as interwoven lancets. When round-headed windows were operable, the window head was frequently square and concealed in an arch-shaped pocket that created the illusion of a rounded head.

Double-hung sash remained popular through each successive wave of 19th-century romantic revival styles that characterized domestic architecture. The Greek Revival style (c. 1820–60) was the first manifestation of this interest in archeologically derived forms, although the windows drew little from antiquity. Like other Greek Revival motifs, windows were built according to established classical designs. In contrast to early Federal-style windows, which tended to be of modest but uniform size throughout a building, Greek Revival windows were larger and usually varied in size from floor to floor. Their proportions, according to an 1844 treatise on the subject, were to "be of different heights in different stories, but of the same width."[5]

The rules of architectural taste dictated window proportion for each story by a specific formula. The first-floor windows, for example, could be nine-over-twelve,

Federal-style row house with six-over-six windows. (Karen Patteson)

the second floor six-over-nine, and the third floor six-over-six. Parlor windows, which dropped to the floor, were especially common on the facades of late Federal and Greek Revival row houses to maximize light and ventilation on the principal floor.

"The sashes of windows," wrote New England architect-builder Edward Shaw in 1831, during the heyday of the Greek Revival, "are generally made of pine, cherry, or mahogany, and sometimes of iron, copper, or other metals."[6] Windows in Greek Revival architecture were boldly delineated, generally with squared heads. Six-over-six, double-hung sash were typical, with lights approximately 10 by 16 inches. Other types found were nine-over-six or even twelve-over-nine. Where larger, full-height openings were required, triple-hung windows were introduced. Smaller windows were placed in entablatures or dormers. Fixed, leaded side and fan lights continued to be used around major entrances.

**The windows of Federal buildings often include fixed, arched transom sash over the front entrance and double-hung, arched sash in dormers. (left), while those of Greek Revival structures frequently are graduated in size from lower to upper floors (right). Front parlor windows sometimes drop to floor level to maximize light and ventilation. (Karen Patteson)**

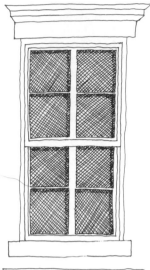

**A thick center muntin in double-hung sash can simulate casement sash. (Karen Patteson)**

The exteriors of windows usually had plain wood or stone lintels with a cap mold. Flat lintels with the top gradually rising to a center point in the form of a pediment were common on residences of the 1830s. Ornamented wood or cast-iron pierced grilles were prevalent in attic or frieze windows. On the interior, windows were framed in molded surrounds that usually matched the surrounds on interior doors and other openings. This trim, often an integral part of the interior architectural scheme, included wainscoting, chair rails, and paneling.

During the Greek Revival period most builders preferred double-hung sash to "French" casement windows. In *The American House Carpenter* (1844), the architect R. G. Hatfield (1815–79) suggested the following formula for designing Greek Revival double-hung sash window frames:

> *To ascertain the dimensions of window frames, add 4 1/2 inches to the width of the glass for their width, and six and one half inches to the height of the glass for their height. These give the dimensions, in the clear, of ordinary frames for twelve-light windows; the height being taken at the inside edge of the still in a brick wall, the width of the opening is eight inches more than the width of the glass—four and one half inches for the stiles of the sash, and three and one half inches for hanging stiles—and the height between the stone sill and lintel is about ten and one half inches more than the height of the glass, it being varied according to the thickness of the sill frame.[7]*

Within a decade row houses began to break from the prevailing Greek Revival style. Originating in rural America, in both elaborate country or farmhouse villas for the wealthy and cottages for the middle class, were new architectural vocabularies borrowed from Roman, medieval, and Elizabethan sources. This led to the popularity of such revival styles as Gothic (c. 1830–60), Italianate (c. 1840–80), and French Second Empire (c. 1860–90). Although these mid-19th-century villas included the same 12-light, double-hung sash seen in Greek Revival dwellings, variations were becoming popular. A profusion of new shapes for window heads appeared. Depending on the style selected, window openings were flat, round, or shallow arched and occasionally pedimented or heavily architraved. Bay windows were very popular; the simplest form was a plain semioctagon with a simple shed roof, but more elaborate versions with complex tracery were also built.

Through his pattern books Andrew Jackson Downing (1815–52) popularized the "picturesque cottage" as an alternative to the Greek Revival style. Intended primarily for rural or suburban contexts, these cottage designs were romantically evocative of earlier European, vernacular buildings, many of which contained the traditional small-paned casement window. Downing wrote in *The Architecture of*

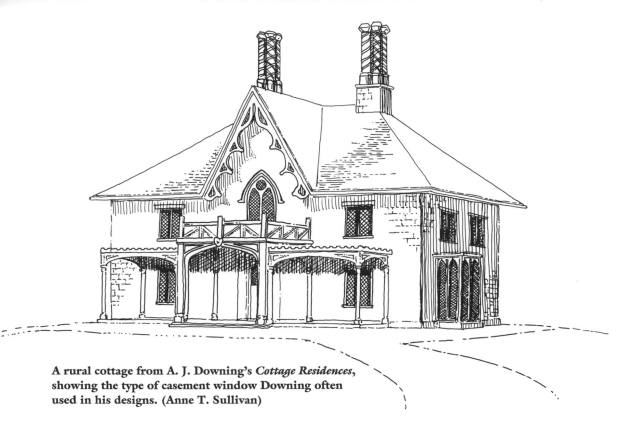

**A rural cottage from A. J. Downing's *Cottage Residences*, showing the type of casement window Downing often used in his designs. (Anne T. Sullivan)**

*Country Houses* (1859) of windows with 12 lights, each measuring 10 by 12 inches, and included diamond-paned windows appearing to be casements in many of his designs. However, the limitations of the casement window, perceived as troublesome and inconvenient, were well known, for they were difficult to weatherproof and secure when open. Downing himself preferred "common rising," or double-hung sash.[8] Many architects and builders achieved a casement appearance by using double-hung sash with a thick center muntin resembling a casement's stiles or by installing a more complicated horizontal sliding sash that could be drawn along a track, sometimes into the wall, when open. Such false casements were frequently used in Gothic, Italianate, Swiss, and English picturesque cottages. For the interior Downing advised simplicity in the treatment of casings and architraves, suggesting widths of up to 6 inches for Italian styles and half that for Gothic.[9]

Many of these rural-inspired details readily found their way into the vocabulary of urban row house facades, where heavy masonry moldings were used with larger or grouped sash to give windows a new appearance and emphasis. Gothic Revival windows were sometimes pointed but more commonly surmounted by wood moldings. Italianate and Second Empire fenestration were usually enframed by elaborate curved architraves. By the late 1840s panes of glass measuring approximately 15 by 30 inches were available in New York City

Gothic Revival window with pointed arched heads. (Richard Pieper)

Gothic Revival wood window with "dripstone-cap" molding.
(Richard Pieper)

30

**Italianate windows often have elaborate architraves of wood or cast iron. (Karen Patteson)**

and used in two-over-two sash or in one-over-one paired elongated sash in finer residences. By 1873 larger sheets of plate glass were available and, according to James H. Monckton, author of *The National Carpenter and Joiner* (1873), typically used in "first class houses."[10]

The proliferation of pattern books was a major factor leading to standard stylistic window details. Architectural pattern books were a popular source of current fashion. Important technological advancements in mill working and joinery as well as an unprecedented expan-

# Official Grades of Sash, Doors and Blinds.

*Adopted by the Wholesale Sash, Door and Blind Manufacturers'*
*Association of the Northwest.*

## DOORS.

AAA. Oil Finish Doors.—Material for AAA. Oil Finish Doors must be Clear, no white sap admitted. Workmanship must be good.

AA. Oil Finish Doors.—Material for AA. Oil Finish Doors must be Clear, with the exception that white sap will be admitted, not to exceed twenty-five (25) per cent of the face of any one piece. Workmanship must be good.

A. Doors.—Material in A. Doors must be Clear, with the exception that water stains and small pin knots not exceeding one-fourth (¼) inch in diameter may be admitted. No piece to contain more than two (2) such defects and no door more than five (5) such defects on each side; white sap not considered a defect. Workmanship must be good.

B. Doors.—Material in B. Doors may contain knots not to exceed one (1) inch in diameter, and blue sap showing on both sides not to exceed fifty (50) per cent in any one piece of the door and gum spots showing on one (1) side of a piece only and other slight defects, shall not exceed ten (10) in number on each side and each white pine stile, bottom and lock rail must contain at least one (1) and not to exceed three (3) such defects; plugs admitted and not regarded as a defect. Slight defects in workmanship admitted.

C. Doors.—Material in C. Doors may contain all stained sap and small worm holes and fine shake; also knots not exceeding one and three-fourths (1¾) inches in diameter. Twenty (20) defects may be allowed on each side, also slight defects in workmanship.

Each piece of white Pine in a No. C Door must contain a defect. Not more than six (6) defects allowed in any one piece.

D. Doors.—D Doors are regarded as a cull door and must contain large coarse knots and may contain rot, worm holes, shake and other serious defects.

A Standard Door may be through tennon, blind tennon or dowelled.

## WINDOWS.

Check Rail Windows may contain two (2) knots three-eighths (⅜) inch in diameter or one red knot five-eighths (⅝) inch in diameter in each piece of a window. White sap and not over thirty-three and one-third (33 1-3) per cent blue sap may be admitted in any one window. Workmanship must be good.

Plain Rail Windows and Sash may contain blue sap and small knots.

## BLINDS.

No. 1. Outside Blinds must be made of Clear lumber, except that small, sound pin knots, water stain and white sap may be admitted. Workmanship must be good.

## WOODS ADMISSIBLE.

Woods other than Michigan, Wisconsin and Minnesota White Pine admitted in Doors, Blinds and Windows, except in Oil Finish Goods.

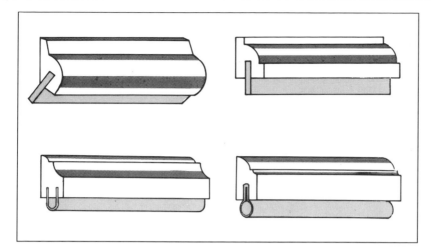

Some early weatherstripping consisted of felt or rubber strips set in slots in wood moldings. (Neal A. Vogel)

sion of urban areas at midcentury created a new demand for mass-produced windows. Mail-order businesses emerged with catalogs containing a diversity of window shapes and styles. Competition eventually brought about a standardization of windows available through catalogs. By the 1880s official grades based on the quality of lumber were adopted by an early trade association, the Wholesale Sash, Door, and Blind Manufacturers Association.[11]

New components were also mass-produced for windows. Wood and felt weatherstrips and storm sash and screens were introduced. Most of these early window types included interchangeable storm sash and screens hung from hooks on the building's exterior, but sliding models were available by the end of the century.

Glazed and screened storm sash frames were made from both softwoods and hardwoods; the screens were of fine wire mesh, painted black to prevent rusting. Interior and exterior blinds were available

Interior vertical sliding blinds of the late 19th century.

Interior folding venetian blinds.

## Special Outside Blinds

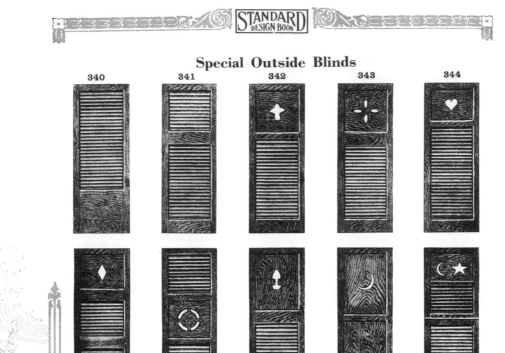

### PRICES OF MODERN FANCY OUTSIDE BLINDS

To arrive at list prices on our special outside blinds (without vent holes cut in panels) add to the list price of a regular outside blind of same size the following list extras, per pair:

| Design No. | | Design No. | |
|---|---|---|---|
| 340 | $1.00 | 345 | $2.11 |
| 341 | .78 | 346 | 1.67 |
| 342 | 1.45 | 347 | 1.89 |
| 343 | 1.67 | 348 | 2.22 |
| 344 | 1.54 | 349 | 1.89 |

The above extras do not include the cutting of vent holes in panels. The various designs of vent holes can be used on any of the paneled blinds. Where blinds have two panels, vents can be cut in both, and in this case the extra for cutting is doubled.

For cutting vent holes in panels of blinds as shown, add to the list price per pair as follows:

| Design No. | | Design No. | |
|---|---|---|---|
| 342 | $0.56 | 346 | $0.89 |
| 343 | .78 | 347 | .44 |
| 344 | .33 | 348 | .33 |
| 345 | .22 | 349 | .67 |

When ordering our special outside blinds, always state clearly the style of blind and design of vent hole wanted. All these blinds are made with stationary slats unless otherwise ordered. Extra wide blinds will be divided with muntins, the same as our regular outside blinds.

Exterior blinds, or "shutters," were made of panels, fixed or movable slats, or a combination of these.

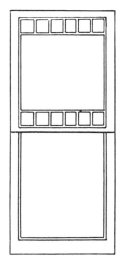 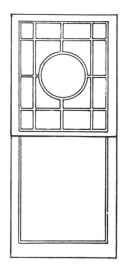 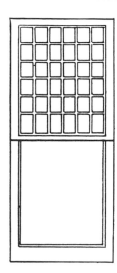

**Queen Anne–style windows typically include fanciful multilight upper sash, sometimes with colored glass in small panes on the perimeter of the sash.**

for ornamentation, shade, or ventilation control. Interior blinds were usually "venetian," made of wood and operated by sliding or folding. Shutters, or exterior blinds, were constructed with panels, slats, or a combination of the two. Cloth or paper window shades on rollers, a popular and less expensive replacement for interior blinds, were available in plain or decorated models.

During the 19th century, interior trim and surrounds for windows were typically well defined, employing continuous moldings and corner or head blocks, often elaborately patterned. Trim was usually built of standard stock, typically 1⅛ inches thick and 4½ to 6 inches wide, and was produced in large quantities from both hard- and softwoods. The exterior trim of the windows varied according to style and material. For masonry buildings, either brick or stone, the openings often had continuous surrounds, pediments, arched lintels, or labels. Moldings were made from brick, wood, or metal, such as cast iron or sheet metal. For frame buildings simple, rectangular molded trim with only a standard drip cap above the head was common. More substantial wood structures, however, used wood exterior trim cut to resemble details found in masonry architecture.

Residential window design underwent a subtle visual transformation in the last quarter of the 19th century. Architects and builders returned to using multiple glazed sash, most of which were variations of double-hung windows, and arranged these to add texture and intimacy to facades. The most distinctive of these was the Queen Anne window, so named because of its association with a popular residential style (c. 1880–1900). The Queen Anne window typically had a multipaned upper sash, usually divided in geometric shapes, and wood or lead muntins above a single glazed lower sash. "Pantry" windows were narrower than other double-hung windows, one or two lights wide and sometimes very tall.

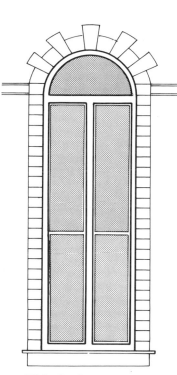

**This slender pantry window fits between pantry shelves in a narrow corridor. (Anne T. Sullivan)**

Windows in the Queen Anne, Shingle (c. 1880–1900), and other late 19th-century "free classic" styles tended to be asymmetrically arranged and often whimsically grouped. These architectural modes also popularized eyebrow, or eyelid, dormer windows, whose sash were either fixed or horizontally pivoting. Fixed or swinging hall, gable, casement, and transom sash, all similar in construction, were introduced along the eastern seaboard in the 1890s and remained in use through World War I. Cottage-front windows had meeting rails placed above the center of the opening, reducing the size of the top sash. These windows were often large, having a top sash of 14 by 40 inches and a bottom sash of 48 by 50 inches. Large cast-iron or even lead weights, which were 80 percent heavier than cast-iron weights, were necessary to counterbalance these large sash.

The most popular and tenacious window style to develop in the late 19th century was the "colonial" window. This window type emerged as fascination with elaborate Victorian decoration waned and interest in classical formalism revived. It marked a nostalgic return of American taste to its own vernacular tradition, sparked by the Centennial Exhibition of 1876 and the beginning of the Colonial or Georgian Revival (c. 1875–present).

Colonial windows, available in period millwork catalogs through the 1940s, were typically wood, six-over-six double-hung sash. Lights in these windows were only slightly higher than they were wide. Sash came in thicknesses ranging from 1⅛ inches, the most common size for plain rail sash, to 1¾ inches; 1⅜ inches was the most common size for check rail sash.

Colonial Revival moldings employed classical motifs. Crown

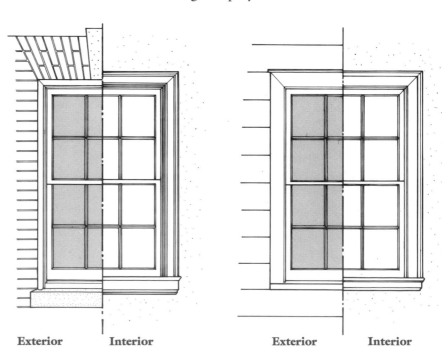

**Colonial Revival windows typically have six-light, double-hung sash. Masonry openings often are surmounted with flat brick and keystones, while simple colonial motifs adorn the exterior window openings of wood buildings. (Neal A. Vogel)**

Exterior   Interior        Exterior   Interior

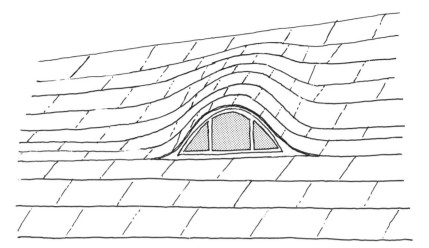

**Eyebrow dormers have fixed or pivoting sash. (Anne T. Sullivan)**

**Cottage-front windows with oversized lower sash.**

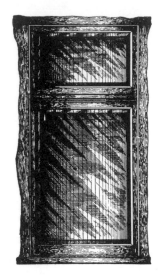

Curved windows made with bent glass were used to special effect in such places as towers and corners.

moldings, cap trim, and fluted trim were typical interior and exterior treatments around windows. Also available was the Palladian window. Unlike earlier moldings, Colonial Revival casing trim was thinner (⅞ inches thick) and usually had no corner or head blocks.

Fancy shapes and new conveniences were introduced in other less common window types in the late 19th century. Curved or bow windows, made of bent glass, were sometimes used to emphasize architectural features such as bays, oriels, turrets, and other rounded forms in complex architectural massings. Aside from curved jambs, sills, and glass, their mechanisms were the same as standard double-hung windows. Reversible double-hung windows equipped with special pivot hardware were introduced to allow easier cleaning. By the end of the century catalogs advertised sash available with both the earlier plain rail and the tighter fitting check, or lip, rail detail.

The earliest multifamily residences in the northeastern United States were tenements. Tenement buildings, which housed up to seven families per floor, neglected adequate lighting and ventilation and for the most part had plain, double-hung sash windows. By the 1870s large multifloored apartment buildings were being built over entire city blocks. Windows used in these buildings were the same as those available for single-family housing and included both wood and metal windows with either fixed or pivoting sash.

In the first decades of the 20th century, improvements in steel making brought about renewed interest in casement windows especially in revival styles. Wood casement windows, available throughout the latter part of the 19th century but still difficult to weatherproof, were used infrequently. Largely because they expanded and contracted less from humidity, steel casements provided closer tolerances than wood and when used with improved hardware were tighter and more delicate in appearance. Metal casements were advertised for use in rural bungalows and city dwellings and, according to a 1914 article in the architectural journal *The Brickbuilder*, "in many modern types of houses which lay claim to no definitive style."[12] Steel casement sash were

Special pivot hardware allow "reversible," double-hung sash to be tilted inward for ease of cleaning.

**Steel casement windows supplanted double-hung windows for much industrial, civic, and urban residential construction early in the 20th century. (Wesley Haynes)**

often combined with pivot and stationary sash to glaze large areas, all divided into smaller panes and lights. This type of window was common in buildings built for artists' studios with northward-facing, oversized windows. Bronze windows, generally made of cast bronze, had excellent fit.

Larger residential structures commonly used kalomein windows, which consisted of wood frames and sash covered with either galvanized steel plate or copper sheet metal, sometimes stamped in ornamental patterns. This type of window, which was also very popular in commercial structures, provided better durability and fire resistance.

VENTILATOR
PROJECTION

**Projecting sash is mounted on pivots in sliding shoes, enabling it to be opened easily and reversed for cleaning.**

As buildings became larger, windows became more difficult to clean. New methods of operation were experimented with to overcome the limits of the counterbalanced double-hung sash. At the turn of the century a "reversible" sash that pivoted around a central point, either horizontally or vertically, was marketed by at least one company for its ease of cleaning.[13] Other window types previously used in industrial buildings were adapted for residential use during the first quarter of the 20th century. Projecting windows combined pivots with a sliding friction shoe to ease the opening of large windows. Austral-balance windows combined two projecting sash with a tie bar, allowing one to swing in and one out. Spring-balance double-hung sash, a variation of the traditional double-hung sash, were equipped with a spring-loaded drum and metal tape instead of pulleys, weights, and chains or rope. All these windows were available in both wood and metal. Frequently more than one type of window or window operation were found in one window opening. Combinations of hopper or transom windows with casement sash were common.

Although such complex window types were frequently used by the 1920s for larger multifamily residences, steel casements were by far the most popular metal sash type. Glazing division followed no fixed rules. English Tudor or Colonial or Georgian Revival apartment facades, for example, usually contained multipaned sash that intentionally recalled earlier window forms. The number of lights typically depended on the architect's preference and the client's budget. By 1930 one-over-one, four-over-four, six-over-six, and six-over-one double-hung windows, as well as multipaned casement windows, were all available in wood and metal and, occasionally, extruded aluminum.

The most common sash in most single and multifamily residences remained the wood, one-over-one double-hung sash. Standard glass sizes ranged from 12 by 18 inches to 36 by 48 inches, in incremental changes of 2 inches. Most double-hung sash were made of pine from North Carolina, Michigan, Wisconsin, or Minnesota. Weatherstripping was widely advertised and available in wood, felt, and rubber, and combinations of the three.

By the end of the 1920s residential windows were extremely eclectic and included various types of fixed, sliding, swinging, and pivoting sash. Folding sash, which allowed for large, clear openings,

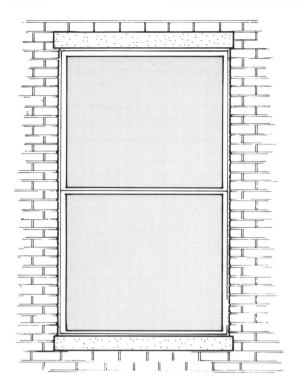

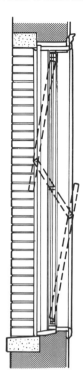

**Austral-balance windows connect projected sash with a tie bar—one sash swings inward, the other outward.**

were also introduced. Colonial windows, windows with divided tops, leaded cottage-front windows, and landscape windows were the most common. The landscape window was a further development of the cottage-front window made possible by the fabrication of even larger glass sheets. This window consisted of a large central section of fixed glass flanked on both sides by small, operable double-hung or casement sash. The arrangement was similar to that of the Chicago windows in commercial buildings, developed in the late 19th century.

Standard-size glass was found in 2-inch increments. Windows were advertised with new patented technologies such as cold-rolled, rust-resisting steel (Fenestra windows), rabbeted check rail sash (Curtis windows), puttyless steel windows (Vento windows), and frames made with interlocking pieces (Fenestra windows). Although aluminum windows were introduced in the 1930s, they did not become popular until after World War II.

After World War II the most significant development in window technology was the use of the aluminum window on a larger scale. Because of its close tolerances, greater emphasis was placed on the technology and its potential to improve performance. Nonetheless, wood windows remain in wide use today in residential buildings.

Window construction in commercial and civic buildings generally followed the same patterns as in contemporary residential structures. While commercial markets and public buildings existed before the 19th century, the growth of American industry and commerce and the establishment of local government and institutions following the American War of Independence created a need for buildings more substantial than residential building types. Commercial and civic buildings, as places of work, public assembly, and sometimes storage, had greater needs to maximize daylight in an era of primitive artificial lighting and protect against fire. These requirements placed new demands on the size and composition of windows.

Beginning in the 19th century civic and commercial buildings were built in monumental styles, first in the Greek Revival style and then in the Roman, Italianate, French Second Empire, Richardsonian Romanesque, and the "American Renaissance," or neoclassical, styles. Like contemporary residential structures, Greek Revival buildings often had windows with squared heads and wood double-hung sash (most commonly six-over-six). By the mid-19th century iron frames combined with metal shutters became common, particularly for civic buildings. Metal shutters were also used in loft or other light industrial buildings. Often a cast-iron front on the street would be combined with cheaper wood windows and metal shutters in the rear.

In the decades following the Civil War many large, load-bearing masonry public buildings were constructed in the Second Empire and Richardsonian Romanesque styles. Their construction necessitated heavy walls, and arched masonry openings were greatly emphasized. Windows were typically set toward the interior of these arches behind deep reveals. Both civic and commercial windows in these styles usually had rounded heads of the same types, but on a larger scale than in residences, as well as swinging casements and sliding double-hung sash with multiple lights.

By the turn of the century one-over-one, double-hung sash were preferred in most commercial and civic buildings in the Northeast. However, as construction technology incorporated the steel frame, the window moved once again to the building's exterior surface. Multiple-light sash were used in many Colonial and Georgian Revival buildings, often equipped with custom swinging or pivoting operating hardware. Variations of the traditional double-hung windows—counterweighted, spring-balanced, counterbalanced, and reversible—were also considered suitable for commercial use.

The need for more durable, fireproof windows in the new larger buildings where maintenance was more difficult prompted a change in materials. By World War I high-rise commercial and civic buildings generally included either steel windows or metal-clad wood windows

**Chicago windows have a large, fixed glass at the center flanked by smaller, operable, double-hung or pivot sash. (Richard Pieper)**

that used copper or galvanized steel. Such windows were noncombustible and thought to be maintenance free. Only 10 years earlier large all-wood windows had still been in standard use.

Cleaning was another maintenance consideration. Specialized hardware for window cleaning was advertised early in the 20th century. Bolt anchors for window washer safety belts were made of cold-rolled bronze and anchored in the masonry or the window framing itself.

Other materials, including cast bronze and nickel silver, were sometimes used, particularly on ornamental features. Because of the monumental scale for such buildings, custom designs were required, and less repetition was likely to be found.

The Chicago window, a development of the late 19th century, originated in Chicago's skyscrapers. It consisted of a large center section of fixed glass flanked on both sides by smaller operable windows for ventilation and was used first in commercial structures.

Steel windows were promoted as increasing natural light and ventilation in office buildings. Framing a window with structural steel permitted larger openings and allowed more than 50 percent of the window to be opened for ventilation while still admitting unobstructed light.

Lupton's Sons Company of Philadelphia made several types of steel windows for commercial buildings, offices, and schools. Their range of products, typical of the time, included projecting sash and counterbalanced, hinged, and pivoted windows. Lupton windows were made of cold- or hot-rolled steel, had standardized pane sizes, and were used into the 1940s with only slight periodic mechanical changes. The windows were made with multilights, and only small sections were operable either as casement or hopper windows.

## WINDOWS IN INDUSTRIAL BUILDINGS

Steel industrial windows take advantage of the large window area allowed by concrete and steel-frame wall construction. Ventilating sash, often located in the center of the window units, have vertical or horizontal pivots. (Richard Pieper)

The American Industrial Revolution began in New England in the first decades of the 19th century and was intensified by the expansion of railroads after 1850. In the following decades the nation's progress was measured by the number of new factories built. Factories dotted the landscape, especially along rail lines and river fronts. Their windows were generally cheaply constructed and typically used double-hung wood sash with glass of a lower quality than that found in residential or commercial buildings of the same time. These multilight windows typically occupied less than 50 percent of the available wall area.

44

Both projected-sash ventilators and steel casement windows were used in this early 20th-century commercial building. (Kim Lovejoy)

By the 1920s the increased use of new construction techniques, including reinforced concrete and steel frames, allowed the ratio of window area to wall surface in industrial buildings to be increased by up to 85 percent. These later windows were mostly of steel, structurally allowing for larger expanses of glass and thus providing improved lighting and offering little obstruction to light. Factory sash were divided into multiple lights and available in a variety of standard sizes in both metal and wood. Some lights were able to pivot or project for ventilation. The use of wood sliding sash in factories was limited to smaller openings, because these required thick mullions in large openings, which blocked light coming into the work area.

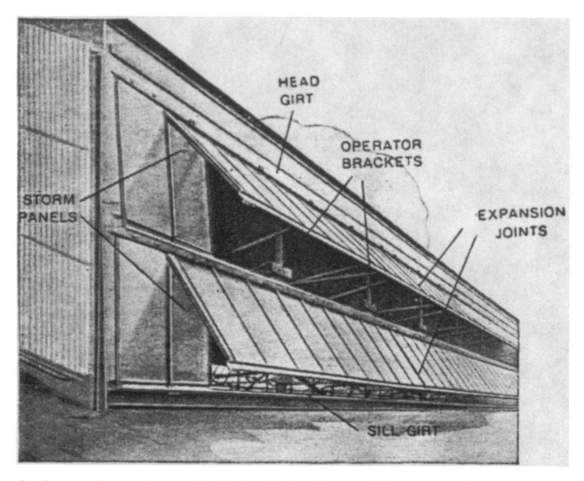

**HEAD GIRT**

**OPERATOR BRACKETS**

**STORM PANELS**

**EXPANSION JOINTS**

**SILL GIRT**

Continuous-sash operation permitted the installation of unusually long spans of windows for light and ventilation in industrial buildings. Often operated with one central-chain mechanism, the windows were easy to operate but provided poor weatherability.

Lupton windows first applied the concept of continuous sash to factories in 1901. Continuous sash were intended as weather-protecting windows and were generally installed in long, unbroken lines from the building's structure. Their weatherability, however, was poor. Fenestra Windows of Detroit manufactured steel continuous sash in four standard heights (3, 4, 5, and 6 feet) for top-hung, center-pivoted or fixed windows, with spans of 8, 12, and 20 feet.

Continuous-sash windows were originally designed for factory roofs. The roof with openings above the line of vision was the best source of unobstructed natural light and at the same time provided an effective form of ventilation without concentrated local drafts.

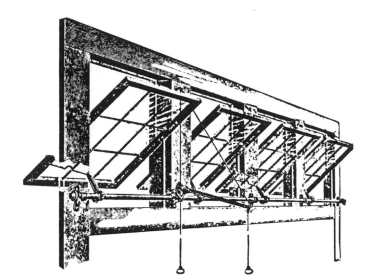

**Industrial horizontal pivot sash are gang-operated by a pull-chain mechanism.**

Mechanical devices were used to open and close both factory and continuous sash. Often they were gang-operated; entire walls of windows could be opened simultaneously with up to 2,000 square feet of vertical sash controlled by hand chains.

With reasonable weather protection and mass control, continuous sash influenced the design of industrial buildings, permitting larger, more pleasant work areas. Extremely wide and long structures, which previously had been almost impossible to ventilate properly and light naturally, could now be built to better serve factories equipped for mass production. The widespread use of the continuous sash and other rolled steel windows in industrial and commercial buildings continued through World War II when the development of the noncorroding aluminum window began to eclipse the use of steel windows.

# 2

# EVALUATING WINDOW CONDITIONS AND PROBLEMS

**M**ore demands are placed on windows than on any other building component. To begin with, windows are functional machines that directly control the interface between a building's interior and exterior environments. Windows admit daylight, fresh air, and pleasant sounds. They exclude rain, temperature extremes, and noise. In addition, windows are key elements of architectural design, organizing the outward appearance of a building facade by their size, orientation, placement, and detail. Windows reinforce the unity of a symmetrically arranged facade or emphasize the picturesque quality of an asymmetrical composition. The division of individual sash by glazing bars, or muntins, further defines the building's character. An undivided window sash boldly delineates solids and voids, while a divided sash adds texture and scale.

There are many reasons to rehabilitate windows, especially those

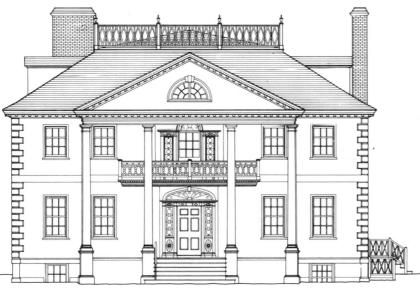

Morris-Jumel Mansion, New York City, c. 1765, a Georgian residence. Georgian and Federal-style buildings have symmetrical fenestration patterns. (Jan Hird Pokorny, Architects and Planners) Opposite:An architect records on a window survey form window conditions requiring repair. (Richard Pieper)

Lyndhurst, Tarrytown, New York, c. 1838. Late 19th-century architectural styles frequently employed a wide variety of window shapes and sizes in asymmetrical patterns. (T. L. Price, Roger C. Erickson, HABS)

Large double-hung windows pose energy conservation problems for the residential conversion of 19th-century commercial and industrial buildings. (Richard Pieper)

in old buildings. Such windows are likely to have been subjected to decades of opening and closing and exposure to seasonal temperature extremes, harsh sunlight, driving winds and rains, and interior condensation. Most windows are designed and built to withstand these forces if properly maintained, like any other machine. When regular maintenance is lacking, windows require rehabilitation.

When a building's use changes, even well-maintained windows often require rehabilitation. Windows in industrial buildings, for example, were generally large to maximize daylight and ventilation for great numbers of workers sheltered within. These original requirements prove problematic when mill or loft buildings are converted to residential use; daylight usually then becomes less important than privacy and energy efficiency. Owners of many old buildings, whether their use is changing or not, rehabilitate windows to improve sound insulation and reduce street noise. In most cases, all these reasons are intertwined. Window rehabilitation encompasses a broad range of measures, from routine maintenance tasks to window replacement projects. These measures vary in cost, performance, and visual consequence. A growing industry—consisting of energy analysts, restoration consultants, window repair contractors, and manufacturers and distributors of weatherstripping, secondary glazing panels, and storm and replacement windows—has developed to meet the growing needs of window rehabilitation. From this seemingly endless shopping list strategic thinking is essential in determining which measure is best for the problem at hand.

Clarifying the project goals from the onset will help cull appropriate measures and develop a sound rehabilitation strategy. The goals of the most successful strategies, and those presented in this manual, include measures that

- preserve the architectural character of the window;
- improve the insulating performance of the window;
- help maintain the window over time;
- are cost effective.

Meeting these goals is a challenge in every rehabilitation project. It is up to the building owner, often with the assistance of a design professional, to set the project goals.

Diagnosing the problem correctly is critical when planning a window rehabilitation project and is best done by an unbiased professional rather than someone selling a particular product or service. These inspection techniques can be used by an owner or do-it-yourselfer to assess conditions on a preliminary basis or to review the work of professionals.

**Large single-light sash contrast strongly with the adjacent wall surfaces. (Richard Pieper)**

## PARTS OF A WINDOW

Windows are machines made up of many stationary and moving parts. In almost all cases a window unit contains glazed sash that

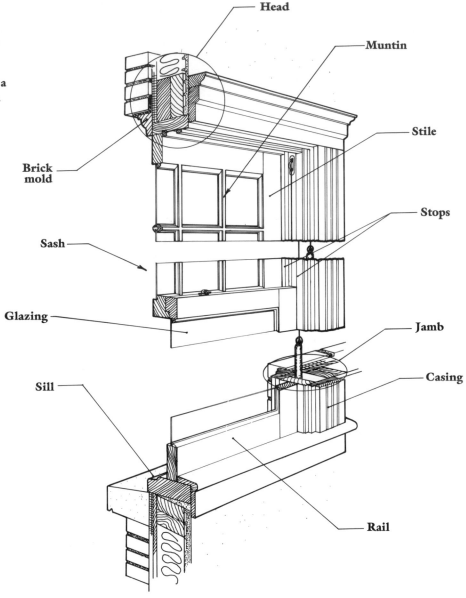

**Sash and frame components of a typical double-hung, six-over-one wood window. (Neal A. Vogel, adapted from a drawing by Jonathan Poore)**

Head

Muntin

Stile

Brick mold

Stops

Sash

Glazing

Jamb

Casing

Sill

Rail

moves by sliding or swinging within a fixed frame or casing. The window unit is placed in a building wall at the window opening. The names and arrangement of wood frame parts differ somewhat in wood and masonry window openings. A window unit has three basic parts: the frame, sash, and hardware.

The frame is the part of the window attached to the building and does not move. The top horizontal section is called the head, or head jamb, and the lower horizontal section is the sill. The part of the frame located on the sides is called the jamb. The jamb includes the small projections called stops that guide the sliding parts and seat, or stop, the swinging parts. The casing is the part of the frame that covers the joints on the interior and exterior where the jamb meets the wall. In old windows the casing is often ornamented with molded millwork. When windows are arranged in groups, the vertical jamb and casing assembly separating them is called a mullion. In masonry buildings the exterior casing of a wood window includes a part called the brick mold where it meets the wall.

The sash is the part that actually carries the glass and moves within the frame. The horizontal parts of a sash are called rails, and the vertical parts are called stiles. The glass in sash is called glazing. Many early sash were glazed with several small panes of glass. Large single panes were generally unavailable before the Civil War, and even when these were available smaller panes were used in many buildings for architectural effect. A sash glazed with more than one pane of glass is called divided-light sash. The small panes are carried and divided within the sash assembly by muntins.

All windows require additional hardware to attach, counterbalance, lock, or otherwise control the movement of the sash. The type of hardware varies depending on how the sash operates. Hardware used in old windows includes hinges, weights and pulleys, latches, handles, weatherstrips, cranks, and extension arms or stay bars.

## TYPES OF WINDOWS

Windows are identified by how the moving parts operate. Four types of windows are commonly found in old buildings and are identified by the movement of the sash: swinging sash, sliding sash, pivot sash, and stationary sash. Windows that contain more than one type of sash operation are referred to as combination sash.

The earliest operable sash in the United States was the casement, or swinging sash, also known as a French window. A casement sash operates like a door. Older casements were mounted vertically to the frame by hinges attached to one of the stiles. Hinges of newer casements are typically attached

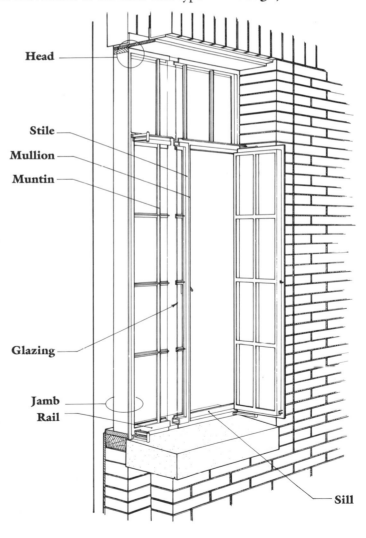

**Components of a typical eight-light metal casement sash with a fixed, four-light transom panel. (Neal A. Vogel)**

Head

Stile

Mullion

Muntin

Glazing

Jamb

Rail

Sill

horizontally to the rails. Wood casements were the predominant window type before the introduction of double-hung sash in the United States in the 18th century. Wood casement sash continued to be used after this, but not until the introduction of the steel casement sash in the early 20th century did it regain widespread popularity.

Wood casement sash are used singly or in pairs. When closed, the top and bottom rails and the hinged stile of a single sash casement seat against a continuous stop set within the frame. When sash are used in pairs, the manner in which the sash meet at the center varies. Where the sash meet, the stiles were typically rabbeted to form a flush profile, coped to form a rounded, or bolection, profile, or lapped with interlocking rabbets. Later paired wood casements were frequently seated against stops of a stationary mullion. Steel casement sash, often called vents, typically meet at a center mullion, called the meeting stile. Hardware for casement sash is relatively simple. In addition to hinges, early casements require some form of metal bolt or latch to secure them shut. Steel and contemporary wood casement sash typically have additional handles, cranks, and stay bars. Sliding sash includes the most widely used traditional type in the United States, the double-hung window. In a double-hung window two sash slide by one another vertically in tracks formed by the stops. The inside stop is called an interior stop. The middle stop is known as the parting stop, parting strip, or parting bead. The exterior stop is called a blind stop. Inside, the bottom rail of the lower sash seats against a horizontal piece, called a stool, that faces the interior and is attached to the sill. Outside the top rail of the upper sash seats against the blind stop of the head.

**Voorlezer's House, Richmondtown, New York, c. 1695, with leaded, inward-swinging casement sash and outward-swinging wood shutters. A glazed transom admits light when the shutter is closed. (Richard Pieper)**

Steel casement sash in 20th-century buildings typically join at a meeting stile. (Mark A. Weber)

Contemporary casements may have stay bars mounted to the interior stool to control sash swing from the interior. (Mark A. Weber)

**In double-hung windows both upper and lower sash slide within tracks on the jambs. (Richard Pieper)**

**In single-hung windows only the lower sash is counterbalanced and operable. (Richard Pieper)**

Variations of this type include the single-hung sash, in which only one sash operates by sliding past a stationary sash, and triple-hung sash, which contain three operable sash. The latter type was frequently used in first-floor openings to provide access onto porches and verandas.

The earliest double-hung sash were not counterbalanced. They

56

**Sash counterweights attached to sash cord or chain typically are accessed through wood panels at the base of side jambs. Panels are screwed in place through a bevel at one end. (Michael J. Devonshire)**

**John Bannister House, Newport, Rhode Island, c. 1756. Triple-hung windows have three operable sash in three sash tracks. The middle window has slender meeting rails at both the top and bottom. (Mark A. Weber)**

were held open by notched spacers or pins that were drilled through the stiles and held in a series of holes in the frame. Counterweights located in recessed weight pockets within the frame are found in windows dating from the late 18th century through 1950. These counterweights are typically attached to the sash by cotton cord or metal chains and operated by a pulley located in the jamb.

Spring-loaded tape balances use flexible, flat, steel tape instead of cords or chains to raise sash. Retractable spring mechanisms are mounted in the head or jambs of the window. (Richard Pieper)

Channel balances keep sash raised with side pressure from springs behind an expanding "parting strip" (the vertical metal strip in the center of the window). (Richard Pieper)

Contemporary double-hung sash are balanced by other kinds of hardware. Spring-loaded tape balances, mounted within the jamb, operate like retractable tape measures attached to the sash. Other balancing systems are mounted on the outside face of the jamb. Channel balances have sheet metal or vinyl tracks with spring-loaded tabs to hold the sash in place. Tube balances are spring-loaded metal or vinyl cylinders that are attached to the top and bottom of the jambs and fit grooves along the sash stiles. Other double-hung sash hardware includes sash fasts, latches mounted on the meeting rails, and handles located on the lower rail of the lower sash to assist in opening.

Tube balances consist of springs in long tubes that are attached to the jambs. Recesses in sash stiles allow sash to ride over the tubes.
(Richard Pieper)

Sash locks secure meeting rails of double-hung windows.
(Richard Pieper)

These Gothic Revival–style horizontal sliding sash slide into recessed pockets in the side jambs. (Anne T. Sullivan)

Another kind of sliding sash rarely used in 19th-century buildings is the horizontal sliding sash. It was intended to look like casement sash but operated along tracks at the head and sill of the opening, sliding into pockets hidden in the wall. Today's horizontal sliders, which are essentially double-hung sash turned on their side, bear little resemblance to their progenitors. The third operational type of window contains sash that pivot on a vertical or horizontal axis. Pivot sash was first used in combination with other sash as vents and transoms, especially in large windows found in religious and industrial buildings. Center vertical and horizontal pivot sash are most commonly found in industrial buildings. They are held open by stay bars, pilot grooves cut through the stops of the frame, or a combination of both.

Bohemian Hall, New York City, c. 1895. This building illustrates the mix of vertical pivot, horizontal pivot, and fixed sash in use by the late 19th century. (Richard Pieper)

**Bohemian Hall, New York City, c. 1895. Large vertical pivot sash are used for second-, third-, and fourth-floor windows. Transom windows are horizontal pivots. (Museum of the City of New York)**

Ornamental stationary sash, such as this elliptical fanlight set in the gable end of a Greek Revival structure, are frequently used to illuminate attic spaces. (Richard Pieper)

This stationary arched sash allows natural light into the attic of a late 19th-century residence. (Richard Pieper)

Awning and hopper sash are other kinds of horizontal pivot sash. An awning window contains sash that is pivoted at the top and opens outward, held in place by a stay bar. A hopper window contains sash that is pivoted at the bottom and opens inward, held in place by a chain.

Stationary sash that does not operate, is the oldest type of window used in the United States. Stationary sash includes primitive translucent mica introduced into the wall to provide light, as well as decorative bull's eye, diaper, and arch-headed shapes typically used in the ends of gables and other remote places. It is also frequently used in combination with other types.

## PHYSICAL PROBLEMS

Once the names of window parts are familiar and their functions are understood, making an initial inspection is not difficult. A careful examination of the windows at the outset will provide important baseline information about window problems.

To organize the task, think about how the window was put together and then conceptually break it apart into its component materials: structural materials (wood, steel, aluminum, glass); finishes (paint, varnish, anodizing); joint material (putty, caulking, weatherseals, sealants, gaskets); and operating hardware (pulls, latches, balance mechanisms, extension arms, sash weights, pulleys).

Many initial questions about setting a course of action for window rehabilitation can be answered in the course of a preliminary visual inspection. The physical condition of the existing windows will set limits on one's approach. This section summarizes how windows deteriorate and identifies the seriousness of various problems. Standard tests are used to simulate or otherwise measure environmental conditions such as water penetration, condensation, conductive loss, and noise infiltration, and descriptions of these are included in the sidebars throughout this chapter. If the building is large or if the conditions encountered are complex, such tests, as well as a more systematic survey conducted by a professional, are in order.

### Deterioration

The parts that make up a window unit begin to deteriorate from the moment the unit is installed. A window straddles two environments, the interior and exterior, which are often extremely different with regard to temperature and moisture content. Window failure begins at the joints, where its different parts meet. If these areas are left unattended, deterioration of the main components themselves sets in.

The primary causes of window deterioration come from three main sources: (1) exterior rainwater driven against exterior surfaces or into the joints of an ill-fitting window; (2) standing rainwater on poorly sloped surfaces; and (3) condensation formed on interior surfaces.

New paint and glazing putty on this restored window keep water from entering window joinery. (Richard Pieper)

Window joints become inoperable, becoming either stuck or deformed, because of poor maintenance practice, notably excessive paint buildup. Other factors beyond the design and construction of the window unit itself cause problems, such as the building's settling or jacking caused by the corrosion and subsequent expansion of structural iron in the window opening.

### Water Penetration and Weathering

Water penetration is the most serious cause of deterioration, jeopardizing both the structural soundness and overall appearance of the window. Deteriorated paint and joint connections between the window jamb and the sill and between the rails, stiles, and muntins indicate water penetration.

The exterior face of the window parts should be in such condition as to resist contact with rainwater and shed it as quickly as possible. Smooth, uniform surfaces and paint coatings, tightly puttied and caulked joints, and the horizontal surface of the sill clearly sloped away from the window indicate that the window is shutting out water. Conversely, rough and irregular paint coatings and surfaces, broken caulk and putty joints, and deflected sills indicate moisture problems.

Leaking windows are likely to damage interior finishes and furnishings as well as encourage possible structural deterioration to the window unit itself and adjacent construction. Controlling water penetration in the window's immediate environment is critical to reducing maintenance costs. Water penetration typically occurs in the same areas of a window subject to air infiltration, especially in the crack perimeter, the joints where the sash meets the sill.

**Air and water infiltration primarily occur in a window's "crack perimeter" (indicated by shading). (Anne T. Sullivan)**

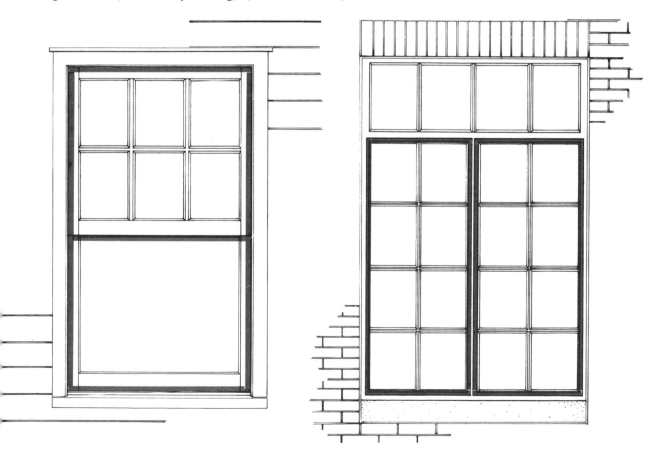

WOOD WINDOWS. Moisture in wood is measured in terms of moisture content, or the weight of water in the wood expressed as a percentage of the same wood when oven dry. The moisture content of green lumber, for example, can be as high as 200 percent before kiln drying, which drops its moisture content to as low as 7 to 10 percent. Particular woods properly used in window and other building construction and maintained for protection from saturation typically have a moisture content of less than 15 percent.

Water saturation in wood windows creates an environment for microscopic fungi. These threadlike plants grow within the wood and attack its cell walls by feeding on them. They generally develop when the moisture content of the wood exceeds 20 percent, thrive where it is 25 percent, and require temperatures below 115°F to be present in an active state. When the fungi are present and active, the wood is considered to be rotting.

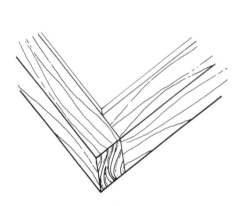

The end grain of wood is more susceptible to rot, causing sash and frame joinery to deteriorate before other elements. (Anne T. Sullivan)

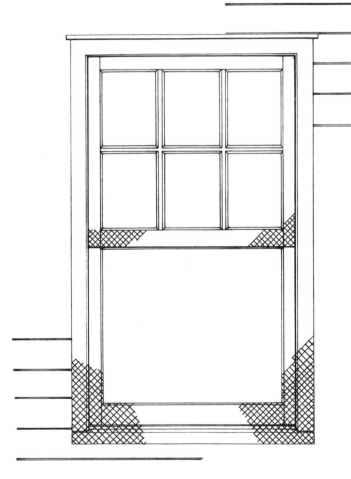

Rot typically occurs first at the joints of jambs and sills and at the stile and lower rail joints of upper and lower sash. (Anne T. Sullivan)

**Water penetration is indicated by interior paint failure on lower sash frame joinery. (Richard Pieper)**

Wood rot is most likely present in a window that has not been regularly painted. When exposed, the end cuts (sections cut across the grain) actually attract moisture into the wood through capillary action and are more susceptible to rot than sections cut parallel to the grain. Rot is predominantly found in the lower third of the window. Sills typically become saturated first as water runs off the other parts of the window and wears away the paint. Moisture is transferred from one wood part to another when they are in contact

67

and will migrate into the lower rail of the sash and the lower sections of the frame. Visual evidence of moisture saturation is the failure of paint on the interior, separation of sash and frame joints, and erosion of the exterior wood surfaces. Controlling moisture on the surface of the sill is the key to solving this problem. If the surface of the sill is rough, it will require more than repainting, for the small depressions caused by the rot will trap droplets of water and continue the process. Rotted sills should be consolidated, or repaired, with two-part wood epoxy system or replaced (see chapter 3). Soft wood tends to absorb water into its endgrain. Moisture absorption is evident when the wood lifts up in short irregular pieces when probed with a pen knife. In many cases this condition can be repaired by consolidating the wood and smoothing its surface to reduce the water's propensity to collect, stand, and saturate the surface. If

**Separation of sash joinery occurs with recurrent moisture penetration. The meeting rail and stile have separated on this arched sash in a church belfry. (Richard Pieper)**

the sill and other horizontal elements are too flat, they should be pitched outward to allow the water to drain off. A snugly fitting sash and jamb and a well-caulked frame will also reduce water penetration.

METAL WINDOWS. Moisture corrodes metal on contact. Unlike wood deterioration, which usually results in a loss of the material's mass, metal corrosion generally results in a slight increase in the material's mass while making it fragile. Steel, like all ferrous metals, rusts during prolonged exposure to the oxygen present in rainwater. Aluminum and copper claddings are also subject to oxygen-triggered corrosion and in addition are susceptible to deterioration from the acids and salts contained in rainwater.

68

**Extreme moisture saturation may result in erosion of wood sills. (Richard Pieper)**

Metal corrosion occurs whenever there is failure of the protective paint or other coating or when moisture finds its way to the inner parts of unprotected metal surfaces, such as those anchored to the wall. Corrosion in steel windows can be controlled by keeping weep holes open in the base of the frame and by scraping and painting the exposed surface. To prevent ponding at the sills aluminum and copper-clad windows should be kept free of dents and an adequate slope on all horizontal surfaces should be maintained.

**Extensive metal corrosion occurred when water leaked behind the outer covering of this copper-clad steel window. (Richard Pieper)**

To evaluate whether the existing window is watertight or whether a method of window repair or replacement will successfully reduce water penetration, a water penetration test can be conducted in the field. In this test the unit is pressurized to simulate a constant wind speed typically 34 miles per hour but frequently higher (60 to 70 miles per hour), depending on the window's height from the ground and its location with regard to prevailing winds. While the window is pressurized, a spray of water equivalent to an 8-inch-per-hour rainfall is directed toward it. If the window does not leak during a 15-minute period, its performance is considered acceptable.

The portable instruments used in testing for air infiltration are used to simulate wind pressures required for this test. On the exterior a spray rack is suspended from the floor above and connected to a water source by a garden hose while the window is depressurized from the interior. The window passes the test if no water is drawn through in the 15-minute period.

**A water spray rack suspended in front of a window is used to test for water infiltration.**

### Condensation

Trapped or standing water caused by condensation either within the window construction or on the sills or surrounding surfaces is another cause of deterioration. Moisture damage caused by condensation is often mistaken for rainwater penetration. When heated interior air, which contains more moisture than cold air, comes into contact with the cooler surfaces of the window, it condenses on those surfaces in the form of small droplets. These droplets eventually find their way down the window's vertical surfaces to its horizontal ones. Condensation is more likely to occur on glass and metal surfaces, which are poor insulators, than on wood. When storm windows are used, condensation is also likely to form on the interior surface of a securely fitted prime (inside) window when cold air leaks around the exterior storm window or on the inside surface of a securely fitted exterior storm window when warm air leaks around the prime window.

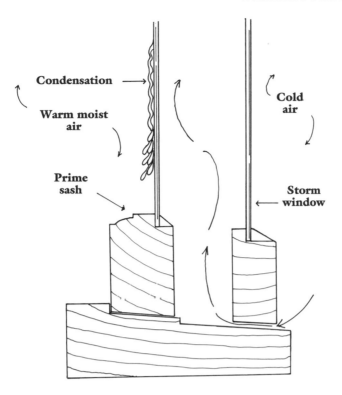

**Condensation**

**Warm moist air**

**Prime sash**

**Cold air**

**Storm window**

When cold air leaks around a storm window, condensation develops on the inside of the prime window. (Michael J. Devonshire)

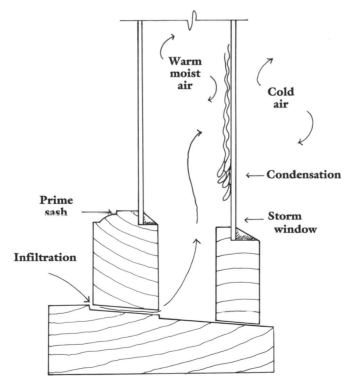

**Warm moist air**

**Cold air**

**Prime sash**

**Infiltration**

**Condensation**

**Storm window**

Condensation develops on the inside of the storm window when air leaks around the prime window. (Michael J. Devonshire)

As indicated by the shaded areas here, condensation damage is most likely to occur on wood sash on the top surfaces of muntins and rails where water condensing on glass will come to rest. (Anne T. Sullivan)

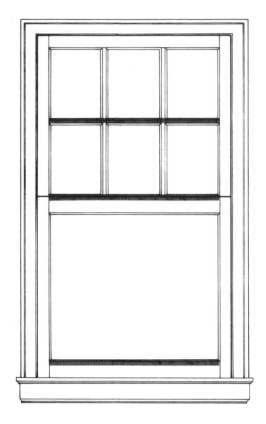

Condensation on metal windows may occur wherever conduction heat loss occurs. In metal windows with thermal breaks, damage occurs in the same horizontal areas as in wood windows. (Anne T. Sullivan)

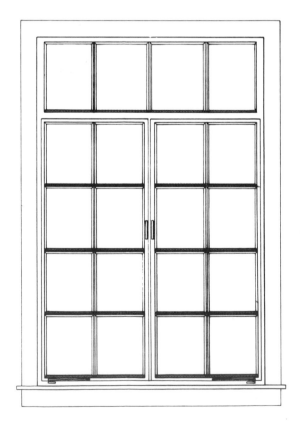

When inspecting windows in warmer months, take into account the building's height and orientation in determining the likelihood of condensation. Condensation is likely to form on tight windows located high above the ground where wind velocity intensifies the cooling of the outside window surface. Windows on different elevations will allow different rates of condensation depending on the orientation and reflection of solar radiation from adjacent buildings. Mechanical dehumidification of the interior spaces should also be noted.

WOOD WINDOWS. Damage from condensation is most likely to occur where the droplets collect—at the bottom points of contact between the glass panes and horizontal muntins and stiles, especially where the exterior glazing compound is in reasonably poor condition.

METAL WINDOWS. All interior surfaces of the sash and frame of metal windows that are not equipped with thermal breaks (see chapter 4) are subject to damage from condensation. In windows equipped with thermal breaks, damage is most likely to occur in the same horizontal areas as wood windows, as well as at any point of the sash and frame that is not insulated by the thermal break.

---

### ASSESSING CONDENSATION

Condensation is a major point to consider when evaluating window rehabilitation strategies. Conditions leading to the formation of condensation should be avoided. An inadequately vented interior storm window, for example, could create condensation by sealing moisture between itself and the sash. Likewise, avoid installing metal replacement windows that are not equipped with continuous thermal breaks at all points of contact between the interior and exterior surfaces.

The condensation resistance factor (CRF), a rating used to measure a material's resistance to condensation, depends on the exterior and interior relative humidity. Interior and exterior air pressure tend toward equilibrium. Thus, a window's CRF is most relevant in winter conditions. A higher CRF rating indicates better resistance to condensation.

---

### Paint Failure

Paint protects window parts from exposure to the elements. It should be thought of as a disposable part of the building, for it gradually exhausts its effectiveness in protecting the wood or metal beneath.

Paint rarely fails evenly over the entire surface of a window. Failure usually begins on horizontal surfaces such as sills, rails, and muntins and spreads to immediately adjacent joints. Most paint failure is accelerated by contact with moisture, but not all failures originate from moisture.

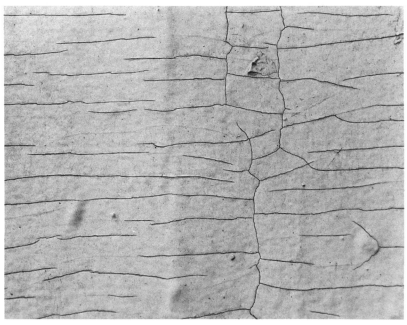

**Paint peels from wood when moisture collects behind the paint. (Richard Pieper)**

**Cracks in paint, which penetrate to the wood, are worsened by moisture penetration. (Richard Pieper)**

Paint failure in windows can be recognized by these common symptoms:

- chalking or powdering of the paint surface, caused by the gradual disintegration of the paint film;

**Alligatoring is a pattern of paint cracking parallel and perpendicular to the wood grain. (Richard Pieper)**

- peeling from wood surfaces, caused by moisture collection behind the paint film;
- peeling between coats of paint, caused by improper surface preparation or incompatible paint types;
- crazing, fine interconnected breaks in the top layer, caused by aging, hardening, and restricted movement of multiple lower paint layers;
- cracking, an advanced stage of crazing, caused by moisture penetration into the crazed surface;
- alligatoring, an advanced stage of crazing in an overall pattern of deeper horizontal and vertical cracks, also caused by moisture penetration; and
- wrinkling and blistering, caused by improper application.

75

**WOOD WINDOWS.** Look for paint failure on the sills that bear the brunt of moisture penetration. If the paint has failed here, look next at the parts of the window in contact with the sill. Failures caused by moisture typically develop first in the lower third of the unit because of a wicking action through the end grain of the wood in contact with the sill. The wood may be damaged in areas exposed to moisture but in many cases can be repaired with consolidants and repainted.

Paint that has failed because of improper preparation or application or too many layers of paint should be removed. If the windows are very old, documenting the existing paint layers is recommended before this removal.

**METAL WINDOWS.** Paint failure is also likely to occur first at horizontal exterior surfaces, especially the sill. Condensation on interior surfaces causes a more uniform pattern of paint failure. In most cases it is possible to scrape off deteriorated paint films, along with any rust, and repaint.

**Racking of the window opening is a structural problem. The new window in this stabilized, racked, brick opening was constructed with an angled head and sill. (Richard Pieper)**

### Window Operation

Each window should be operated in the course of an inspection. A window that does not fully open and close as originally intended should be considered to be in poor operating condition. Many of these conditions stem from poor maintenance rather than inherent design flaws or poor physical condition and are easily corrected. Others indicate physical deterioration requiring costlier repair or even replacement.

A double-hung sash in proper working order should provide 50 percent ventilation of the entire window opening when open and be relatively easy to operate. The sash should fit snugly in the tracks formed by the stops and not be too loose or tight. If a sash is stuck, check the condition of the paint film between the sash and frame. Excessive paint buildup, typically found in the upper sash, is a common cause. Deformed weatherseals or intentional caulking for energy conservation reasons are other causes. All these problems are relatively easy to correct by removing the paint film, weatherseal, or sealant. Another cause of an inoperable sash is severe racking or deflection in the frame, a less common but more serious problem. This should be evident by a lack of rigidity in the parallel parts of the sash and frame members. Racking of the frame indicates a structural problem in the wall that should be investigated by a structural engineer. Racking of the sash in a rectilinear frame or wall opening is most often due to the failure of the joints connecting the sash stiles or rails. In this case the sash will feel loose to the touch on operation and will require extensive repair or replacement after the structural problem has been corrected.

A sash that is stuck because of warping usually requires replacement. If the sash is so loose that it will not stay in place, first check the condition of the counterbalance mechanism and stops. Replacing broken ropes or chains that typically carry old wood sash is a simple repair job. Problems with more complex counterbalance mechanisms are more difficult to correct. Realignment of loose or worn stops is also complicated but often possible and economical. If the corner of the sash has lost some of its original mass through wear or deterioration due to moisture, it does not necessarily require replacement. The difference can frequently be made up by adding weatherstripping or rebuilding the edge of the sash.

A casement sash in proper working order should provide 100 percent ventilation of the entire window opening when open. Most casements depend to a certain degree on hardware to operate and keep them in place. Excessive paint buildup or grime on casement hardware is frequently the cause of sluggish operation. Cleaning with solvents and regular oiling of moving parts will solve this problem. Casements are sometimes painted or caulked in place; once again, removal will permit operation. It is more common for excessive paint buildup, sealants, or deformed weatherseals to render the sash loose at the crack perimeter. Removal of these coats of paint usually allows the casement to fit in the frame as originally intended. As with double-hung sash, racking of the window opening results in either stuck sash or poorly fitting sash. Deformation of the frame is common in steel casements because of jacking caused by corrosion between the frame and wall.

## Analyzing Windows

If the preliminary inspection signals the need for rehabilitation, a systematic survey is strongly recommended. The survey should be methodical and comprehensive in recording the conditions observed. The survey is not an end in itself but a useful tool in the planning process to identify patterns of conditions for further analysis and material quantities for the purpose of budgeting. Depending on the level of detail, information collected in the course of a survey forms the basis for competitive bidding and contract documents. When the replacement of architecturally and historically significant windows is necessary, a survey can substantiate conditions at a level required by preservation agencies.

Techniques for conducting window surveys vary according to the needs of the specific project. A typical survey identifies the number of windows and their sizes, shapes, materials, glazing divisions, method of operation, and physical condition. On smaller buildings it is often possible to survey each window, but typically on larger buildings sample representative windows are tested for the survey.

The survey process is greatly expedited when the drawings of the building's elevations and typical window types are available and are used. It is more convenient and accurate to note conditions on drawings than to describe them in words. In some cases visual inspection is adequate to establish a course of action. Other projects benefit from additional research, physical investigation, and field measurements of simulated environmental conditions.

When restoration of the building to an earlier appearance is a goal of the project, research is essential. Sources to be consulted include such materials as landmark designation reports, building records, historical photographs, drawings, and written descriptions.

A certain amount of probing with simple tools usually assists in the analysis of conditions. Generally this probing will involve using a pocket knife, wire brush, or other readily available tools. A pocket knife, for example, may be used to determine the condition of wood by first removing any scaling or peeling paint and subsequently by prying up small sections of wood to determine whether it is structurally sound or deteriorated. The condition of putty and sealant may also be determined in this manner. A wire brush or other scraper can be used for steel-framed windows when extensive corrosion has covered the metal. In this case it will be important to determine how much of the original metal cross sections remain.

Certain aspects of a window's performance, especially energy and sound insulation, cannot be determined by visual inspection. Tests using portable instruments are used to measure and record actual rates of air and noise infiltration. In addition to standard calculations to determine thermal properties, these tests can present a fairly accurate description of the performance of an existing window and suggest specific areas where cost-effective solutions should be sought. Field tests conducted by professionals to determine energy and acoustic performance are described in the sidebars of later sections.

### Visual Inspection

Most visual inspections are conducted from the inside of the building but include all components of the window, including those on the exterior. The windows should be examined carefully, taking into account fit, extent of deterioration, ease of operation, and to some extent appearance. Crucial is the examination of the physical condition of the various materials making up the window system, including paint finishes, evidence of rot or corrosion, tightness of joints (caulking, sealants, and glazing compounds), and operation of the window (the hardware, sash weights, pulleys, and so forth). When the window systems are more specialized, the assistance of a restoration architect or experienced contractor is advisable.

In general, inspect at close range the condition of the closure between the wall opening and window frame, between the window frame and sash, and between the sash themselves. The condition of caulking, sealants, weatherstripping, and glazing gaskets should be noted. The structural soundness of the sash and frame, the condition of the glazing, and the operation of the window and its hardware should also be inspected. Illustrations on this and the next page summarize many of the conditions likely to be encountered in old windows. During the inspection it is important to note the number of glazing layers and type of glazing in the window. Moreover, the interior surfaces surrounding the window and the materials of the window should be inspected to determine whether water damage has occurred. This problem is likely to be found in spaces where high humidity levels are present, such as kitchens and bathrooms.

**Typical deterioration problems of hung wood windows. (Anne T. Sullivan)**

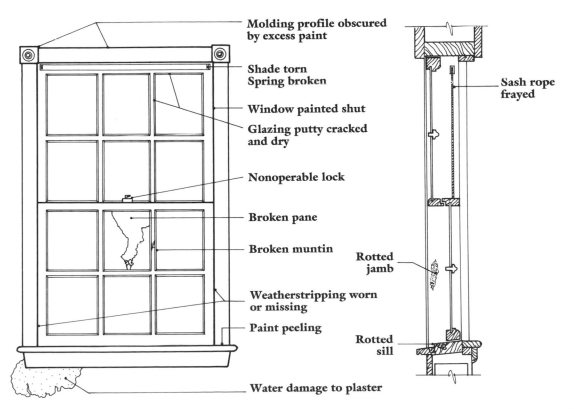

Molding profile obscured by excess paint

Shade torn
Spring broken

Window painted shut

Glazing putty cracked and dry

Nonoperable lock

Broken pane

Broken muntin

Weatherstripping worn or missing

Paint peeling

Water damage to plaster

Sash rope frayed

Rotted jamb

Rotted sill

79

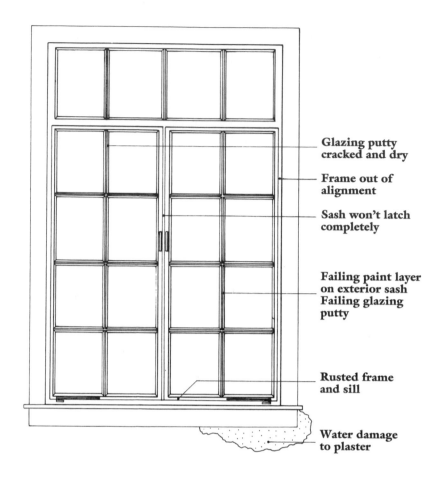

Glazing putty cracked and dry

Frame out of alignment

Sash won't latch completely

Failing paint layer on exterior sash
Failing glazing putty

Rusted frame and sill

Water damage to plaster

The exterior conditions of windows are often difficult to inspect. On small buildings they can be clearly seen from the ground or a ladder. Taller buildings may require the use of field glasses from the ground or from adjacent buildings. In some cases it may be advisable to engage a scaffolding contractor to install and operate temporary suspended scaffolding to allow an inspection of one or more sample surveys, or "drops."

### Assessing Energy Performance

Energy performance in most old buildings tends to be determined largely by the effects of heating and cooling on the envelope or skin—namely, the exterior walls, windows, doors, and roof. These "skin-dominated" buildings were designed before the era of interior environments controlled by mechanical means such as fans and cooling systems, and windows thus account for a large proportion of the building's energy loss through its skin.

Other factors, however, inherently help maintain a thermal balance in the skin of an older building. Massive, load-bearing masonry walls, for example, possess positive insulating characteristics, and this fact should be carefully considered in developing a rehabilitation strategy. Determining the nature and extent of the window's energy loss is a prerequisite in assessing its rehabilitation potential. It has been estimated that windows in houses typical in the northern half of the United States are responsible for 15 to 35 percent of the building's total heat loss in winter. Energy is typically transferred through a window in four ways: infiltration, radiation, conduction, and convection. The careful inspection of windows can identify areas of energy loss, and the extent of such losses can be roughly quantified by an energy analyst using standard calculations. More precise measurements can further be derived from field testing with portable instruments similar to those in product-testing laboratories.

### Air Infiltration

In old buildings the most easily identified and often the most serious energy problem stems from air infiltration. Infiltration is the leakage of outdoor air into the building. Energy loss through infiltration occurs when heated or cooled air in a building is replaced by unconditioned air entering through cracks and holes in the building's skin. This air must be heated or cooled in order to maintain the controlled temperatures inside, a process requiring additional energy. If the amount of air infiltration is excessive, energy used to condition this air is wasted.

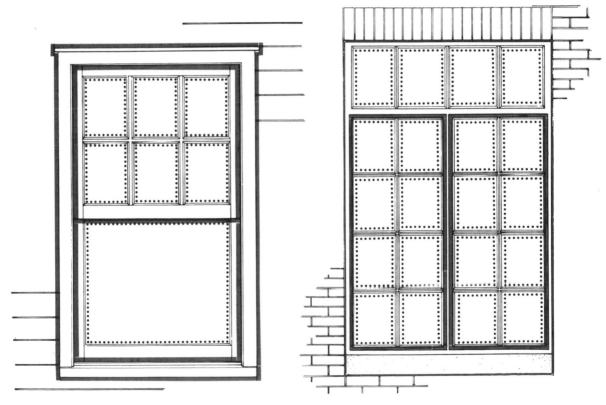

**Air infiltration in double-hung wood windows. (Anne T. Sullivan)**

**In metal casement windows air infiltration occurs primarily at the periphery of the sash. (Anne T. Sullivan)**

66849

Missing caulking where a wood window frame meets a masonry wall may be a major cause of air infiltration. (Richard Pieper)

To admit light, provide a view, and in most cases allow for natural ventilation, windows require an opening in the wall that is filled with glass and other dissimilar materials. As a result, it is subject to air leakage. These air infiltration leaks are most likely to occur in locations where dissimilar materials meet or where complex operating parts meet. Illustrations on page 81 indicate where infiltration losses are likely to occur. A window that fits loosely because of insufficient maintenance, for example, is susceptible to increased energy loss. Infiltration is likely to occur at these junctures:

•where the window frame meets the wall;
•where the operable sash meets the frame or other sash members;
•where the glass panel meets the sash; and
•at sash-weight pockets.

Infiltration can occur where building movement or warpage of materials causes the wall and the window frame to separate and the caulking to fail. Damaged or missing caulking at this joint is a primary cause of infiltration. Older buildings often used caulking materials of limited life span, such as oakum (horsehair) or lead putty. These caulks are now obsolete except in the most exacting restoration projects.

During the inspection the condition of the caulking material on the building's exterior should be checked. Note the length of the joint that is missing caulking or that has opened up to allow the passage of air into the building's interior. Although only small sections may be missing caulking, recaulking the windows completely will probably be necessary for long-term durability as well as compatibility between new and existing caulking. Also note the condition of the joint between the window frame and the wall on the building's interior and make note of any areas open to the wall cavity or directly to the exterior. Check that the frame fits properly in the wall and note any warped or bent members. In cases where warping is limited, moderate-sized gaps can be filled with neoprene or other backing material and caulked over.

The crack perimeter, as noted earlier, is the total length of the crack between sash and frame and other sash in an operable window. In a double-hung sash the crack perimeter is three times the width plus two times the height. In a single casement window it is two times the width plus two times the height. In a double casement window, which meets at a mullion, it is three times the height plus two times the width. In combination sash it varies. The longer the total crack perimeter, the greater the risk of air infiltration.

Infiltration is present in loose, improperly fitted, broken, warped, or missing sash or frame members. Inoperable hardware, such as broken or missing locks, bent hinges, or broken cranks, pivots, and balances, also prevents the sash from closing and fitting tightly into the frame. Damaged, deteriorated, or partially missing weatherstripping can also create a path for infiltration.

Inspect the sash where it meets the frame and other sash. Note areas where these parts do not seal tightly. Check the jambs, head, sill, rails (in double-hung windows) and stiles (in casement windows) and note the condition of the stops. Operate the window and note the condition and type of hardware used, including locks and latches. Performing neglected maintenance, such as removing excess paint buildup, and installing weatherstripping are measures that can reduce infiltration along the crack perimeter.

Cracked, broken, or missing glazing is a source of air infiltration. Less obvious but equally critical leakage occurs around the pane when glazing compounds and sealants are damaged or missing. The greater the number of individual panes in multiple glazed sash, the greater is the risk of air infiltration. A one-over-one sash, for example, minimizes the total perimeter of the glass's interface with the sash.

Note broken and cracked panes. Inspect each window pane and note areas where the glazing compound is cracked, missing, or separated from the sash. Replacement of broken glass or reputtying will often eliminate infiltration here.

In certain window types, especially those with wood and metal double-hung sash, pockets in the wall for sash weights and other operating mechanisms can be a source of leakage. This leakage is either due to problems inherent in the detailing or pulley openings or caused by shrinkage or missing pocket doors. This condition is exacerbated when the frame is inadequately caulked. Inspect the pockets in the wall and jamb for loose or missing covers or openings to the building's exterior. Make note of the typical construction of the pocket interiors to determine whether there is sufficient room or need to apply insulation at this location. The installation of pulley covers also can reduce infiltration losses.

### Conduction

The materials in a wall impede the flow of heat into and out of a building by providing resistance to the flow of energy. A wall's resistance, or R-value, is a measure of the insulating qualities of the materials of which it is made. In general, the R-value of an opaque wall is higher (i.e., the wall is more resistant) than the R-value of a window assembly. The transmission of heat through materials is measured by U-values, the inverse of R-values.

Conductive heat loss is caused by heat flowing out of the building through the materials that make up the building envelope. The less resistance to heat flow that an assembly has, the greater will be the heat loss due to conduction. Windows are a source of conductive heat loss because of their low resistance to heat flow. Illustrations on page 85 show where conductive heat losses are likely to occur in single-glazed windows. The following conditions contribute to the greatest conductive losses:

- single glazing;
- conductive metal frame and sash members;
- water-soaked wood frame and sash members; and
- frame and sash members when the dimension of the material has been reduced by rot.

Single glass with a U-value in the range of 1.10 to 1.23 provides little resistance to heat flow. During the inspection note the number of glazing layers in the sash. By adding an additional layer of glazing material to the sash, an insulating layer of air can be created. The thickness of the sash and members and muntins must be measured to determine whether the sash can accept, or be altered to accept, the added glazing layer. The existing sash needs sufficient material to create an air space and introduce a rabbet deep enough to carry the

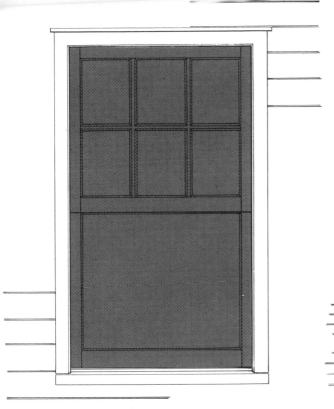

In wood sash, conductive heat loss occurs primarily through single glazing. Some heat loss also occurs through wood-frame members at the window perimeter. (Anne T. Sullivan)

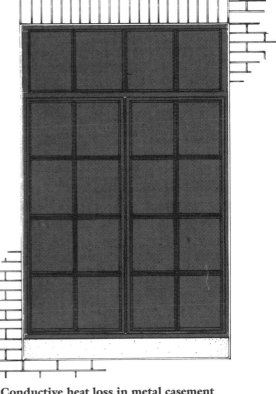

Conductive heat loss in metal casement windows occurs both through glazing and through metal-frame and sash members when no thermal break is present. (Anne T. Sullivan)

weight of the glazing material. Sash weights or balance mechanisms and hinges must also be inspected to determine whether they can be adapted to handle the additional load. Note the existence and condition of storm windows, blinds, drapes, shades, and shutters on the window. These items also can contribute substantially to increasing the window opening's resistance to conductive heat flow and minimizing the problems encountered with single glazing.

Metal has a very low R-value. Metal window sash and frames constructed without a thermal break provide a direct path for heat to flow out of the building. To resist this flow, a plastic thermal break is introduced to separate the metal's exterior and interior faces. When no thermal break exists, condensation on the inside will be an indication of direct heat transfer. Also, when inspecting old replacement windows, it is important to determine whether the original thermal break remains structurally sound. Earlier plastic thermal break materials may have cracked, no longer securing the window or sash front to back. Look for a separation developing between the interior and exterior of the frame and sash members.

Inspect the window frame and sash materials. Thin metal profiles, both aluminum and steel, are probably not equipped with thermal breaks. The frame materials will affect any calculations made of heat loss through the window.

Wood is a good insulator and has a relatively high R-value. Water-soaked wood that is unprotected and exposed to weather, however, has a reduced R-value because of the increased conductivity of moisture. Inspect the finish of wood window members. Probe gently with a knife and note areas of wood that are unprotected and show signs of water damage. As previously noted, such damage is closely related to the window's physical condition. When the frame material has lost mass because of rot, corrosion, or wear, or when the window's detailing has been reduced, conductive heat loss will be greater than necessary. These conditions may also indicate structural failures in the window system. Note any areas where the window frame or sash material has deteriorated or been removed and determine whether these areas are of immediate concern. Check particularly the lower portions of the sash and frames, where water has a tendency to collect.

## MEASURING CONDUCTIVE LOSS

Windows lose heat by conduction through the window frame as well as through the glass. Metal-frame windows in particular experience heat loss through the frame. The loss of heat through the frame is calculated or taken from a table giving the U-value of the materials from which the frame is constructed. This value is translated as the percentage of the area of the window occupied by the frame and is then incorporated into the thermal transmittance of the window as a whole. Unless the frame is steel, which offers no resistance to heat transmission, it provides some level of reduction in thermal transmittance. The frame factor and its effect on the window's U-value establish a basis for comparison when considering the energy savings of a change in window frame or sash material.

A window's location in a building affects its conductivity. In their 1974 study *Windows: Performance, Design and Installation,* authors Beckett and Godfrey categorized window exposure by localized environmental conditions.[1] In buildings in an urban center windows of the first through the third floors are said to be sheltered. Windows of the fourth through the eighth floors experience normal conditions, and windows above the eighth floor are subject to severe conditions.

Air space between glass is a significant factor in reducing U-values. Following is a breakdown of the effects of exposure

## Radiation

Heat loss and especially heat gain also result from radiation. Since windows contain transparent or semitransparent materials, heat can be radiated through them, into or out of the building. Radiation is a significant problem when a building is mechanically cooled. Heat from direct sunlight shining directly into a building can add considerably to the cooling load. Heat radiated out of the building at night or on dark winter days is a less significant problem but still worth considering, especially in climates with severe winters. The transparency of glass and lack of adequate shading contribute to energy losses through radiation. Illustrations on page 88 indicate where radiation is likely to occur in windows.

The primary cause of radiation losses or gains is inadequate shading of the glazed area. This problem results from missing or unused awnings or from a total lack of shading control. Make note of the type and condition of window treatments, including shades, shutters, drapes, blinds, awnings, and overhangs (such as reveals and eaves). When inspecting older windows it is important to investigate whether

on the U-values of single-glazed windows as well as a comparison of U-values for varying amounts of air space in double- and triple-glazed windows.

Under sheltered conditions a single-glazed window with a U-value of 5.0 transmits 44 percent more heat than a double-glazed window with an air space of either ½ or ¾ inch. Under normal conditions a single-pane window increases its transmission of heat to a U-value of 5.6 and correspondingly transmits 46 percent more heat than a window with double panes spaced ½ inch apart and 48 percent more heat than a window with double panes spread ¾ inch apart. Under normal conditions 62 percent more heat is lost through a single-pane window than through a window with triple panes spaced ½ inch apart. Sixty-four percent more heat is lost than in a window with triple panes spaced ¾ inch apart. This is only a 2 percent greater savings, negligent in most cases when compared to the added cost of triple glazing.

Under severe conditions single-glazed windows above the eighth floor have a U-value of 6.7, transmitting 50 percent more than a window with double panes spaced ½ inch apart and 52 percent more heat than a window with double panes spaced ¾ inch apart. The single-glazed window transmits 67 percent more heat than a window with triple panes ½ inch apart and only 68 percent more than a window with triple panes spaced ¾ inch apart.

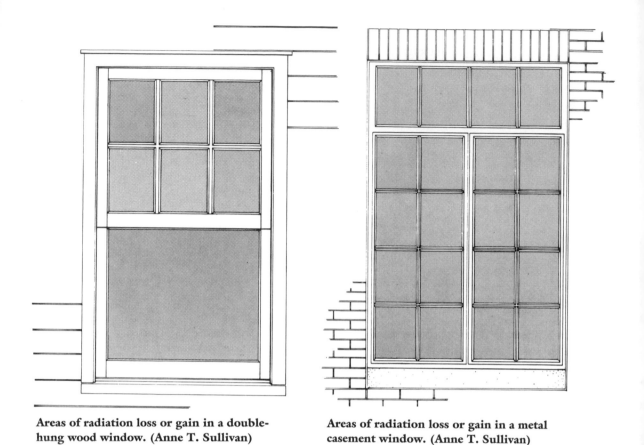

**Areas of radiation loss or gain in a double-hung wood window. (Anne T. Sullivan)**

**Areas of radiation loss or gain in a metal casement window. (Anne T. Sullivan)**

the windows originally had shading devices, such as awnings, shutters, or shades, which were once quite common and effective. Also note the usage patterns and frequency of operation of the shading device. If no shading is currently used on the window, note the surrounding details on the inside and outside of the building to determine whether a shading device can be installed or whether shading by adjacent trees or tall buildings can be used to advantage.

### Reducing Radiation Losses and Gains

Radiation losses and gains are not simple to estimate or to present as a fixed quantity for comparison. The impact of radiation losses and gains on a space's energy performance depends on the conditions being maintained, the type of surfaces in the space (which may or may not absorb solar radiation), and such issues as the occupancy schedule, building use, and so on. In general, radiation should be considered in evaluating a rehabilitation strategy when one or more of the following conditions are present in the building:

• the space is mechanically cooled;
• particularly light-sensitive materials, such as historic fabrics or paper, are located near sunny windows; or
• the building is in cold climate and is heated at night.

Shading the window opening to reduce solar gain and the effect of radiation on materials should be considered primarily for windows facing south and secondarily for windows facing east and west. Methods for shading a window include awnings, interior or exterior shades and shutters, curtains, drapes, overhangs, certain applied films or special glazings, and deciduous trees. The use of a shading device consistent with the building's historic character is preferable.

The value of the shading strategy can be evaluated by measuring the room temperature before and after implementing the shading device. Both cooling and insulation values should be considered in light of the historic context, the required maintenance, and the aesthetic impact of the shading system. Shutters are an example of a shading device appropriate to several modes of architecture. If shutters in a style appropriate to the building's architectural style are selected, they will reduce heat loss at night and heat gain in the summer without appearing aesthetically obtrusive. Exterior shutters can be used effectively with double-hung windows and inward-swing casements. If the building is located in a historic district, the surrounding buildings also may influence the owner's decision regarding the appropriateness of awnings or shading for reducing radiation gains and losses.

Shading the window opening to reduce heat radiation to the night sky should be considered for all windows when this form of heat loss is significant to the building's energy consumption. Shades and drapes that are closed at night (and thus contribute to a reduction in conductive losses) can be used to reduce night radiation while still permitting the beneficial admission of solar radiation during the day, when they are opened.

**Unrealized Potential**

Another way in which energy consumption can be reduced is using all the energy potential of a building's windows. Investigating this potential is important because this may be a way to reduce energy costs with minimal capital expenditure and yet more cost effectively than through extensive rehabilitation.

The transparency and operability of windows allow for natural light and ventilation to supplement mechanical ventilation and electric lighting. Most buildings constructed before the period 1910–15 were designed with natural lighting and ventilation of the building a high priority. This potential should be at least retained and certainly exploited to reduce energy consumption. Poorly functioning operable windows and obscured glazing are examples of unrealized potential.

Inoperable, broken, or sealed windows that cannot be opened eliminate the potential for natural ventilation during temperate weather. Make an attempt to operate all the windows (excluding stationary sash); note those that are difficult or impossible to open and indicate the reasons. Keep in mind that in certain situations, particularly in controlled environments such as museums or computer rooms, uncontrolled use of natural light and ventilation may not be desirable.

When window glazing is obscured by opaque materials or paint, the opportunity to use natural lighting to reduce electrical consumption is wasted. Excessive dirt accumulation may also be a cause of opacity. Inspect the window's glazing. Also note whether the electric lighting in a space can be independently controlled to capitalize fully on this natural light potential.

## NOISE INFILTRATION

Old windows can be a major source of noise infiltration, a growing problem in urban areas. Noise insulation requirements have not been fully developed in the United States, although the subject is under study.

The dynamics of noise infiltration are similar to those of air infiltration and conduction, and the physical conditions of windows that contribute to these energy issues are also similar. If a window is equipped with single glazing and is loose at its crack perimeter, it probably allows the infiltration of noise.

---

### MEASURING NOISE INFILTRATION

Sound transmission class (STC) is measured in terms of decibels (dBA). The STC represents a single-figure rating based on the amount of sound transmission lost in a window that is exposed to noise of various frequencies. The greater the STC, the greater the acoustical insulation is and the smaller the amount of noise infiltration. Noise infiltration is measured in the field by mounting a sound source on the exterior or source side of the test window and measuring the noise reduction with instruments on the interior, or receiving side.

---

## OTHER REHABILITATION CONSIDERATIONS

Developing a rehabilitation strategy does not end with the analysis of the window's potential itself. The next step is to place this analysis within the broader context of other needed rehabilitation work on the building, anticipated maintenance requirements, and the specific local regulatory framework.

The following questions should be answered in the course of developing a window rehabilitation strategy:

• Is the building a designated landmark, or is the project seeking certification for an income tax credit (ITC)?
• What is the extent and sequence of other rehabilitation work being done on the building?
• Will the building be occupied when the windows are rehabilitated?

• How will the building be maintained following its rehabilitation?

• What is the maximum anticipated budget for the project?

### Historic Preservation Regulations and Other Codes

If the building is locally designated as a landmark, contact the local preservation agency and request copies of applicable regulations. If the building is listed in the National Register of Historic Places and the project is seeking certification by state and federal agencies for an ITC, review the Secretary of Interior's Standards for Rehabilitation (pages 161–64) and contact the state historic preservation office (SHPO) for information on current policy. Review these requirements before starting any work. For additional information on landmark buildings, consult chapter 5.

Mandatory energy codes may also be applicable in certain locales or as part of the requirements of loan and tax incentive programs. These requirements also should be thoroughly reviewed (contact the local building department).

### Extent and Sequence of Rehabilitation Work

Outline all other rehabilitation work contemplated for the building so that window rehabilitation can be coordinated with other construction activities. Coordination is essential to prevent delays and protect completed work. Window rehabilitation usually involves opening the building to the elements. In some cases it requires structural work on the building's walls. In general exterior masonry work, such as cleaning and repointing, should precede window work, and interior finishing should follow it. Work items requiring scaffolding should be carefully sequenced.

Window rehabilitation in any project tends to require a great amount of time. Rehabilitating existing windows in a large building is usually done by a small crew at a slow rate over the course of the entire project. Replacement windows, on the other hand, require substantial advance time for construction and delivery.

### Building Use and Occupancy

Occupancy of the building at the time of rehabilitation directly affects scheduling and the way the work can proceed. Rehabilitating windows in an occupied work space can be disruptive to office efficiency. In an occupied living space it can be a nuisance. If the building will be occupied at the time of window repairs, the window work may need to be done during off-hours or handled room by room or floor by floor rather than by window type or exposure. Greater latitude exists in unoccupied buildings. As a result, the cost of rehabilitating an occupied building is usually greater than that of a vacant building.

Although these considerations are generally the contractor's responsibility, prepare an occupancy schedule for the building during rehabilitation. It will be useful when selecting and estimating the costs of a rehabilitation strategy.

### Continued Window Maintenance

Deferred or inconsistent maintenance procedures are often a direct cause of window deterioration. A window rehabilitation strategy must be selected with the procedures required to maintain the windows in mind. What kind of manpower or staffing will be available to maintain the rehabilitated windows? Whether the windows require minor rehabilitation, extensive repair, elaborate retrofitting, or complete replacement, they will require some maintenance to continue working properly. Review the availability and qualifications of personnel to carry out these maintenance tasks. If additional staff or regular service contracts are required, include these items in the budget.

### Budget

Establish a realistic budget. The availability of funds is usually the greatest limiting factor in determining the scope of the rehabilitation. Selecting what necessary work will be done with the available resources should be based on a thorough understanding of the building conditions and available options.

Outline the sources and amount of funding available for the project. Also identify tax incentives that may be applicable and the regulations associated with them. When resources are limited, careful scheduling and phasing may be required.

### REHABILITATION STRATEGIES

Following the analysis of the windows' condition and environmental performance, the final step in the planning process is determining strategy. As previously noted, this strategy also must take into account the visual, architectural, and historical importance of the existing window. Several rehabilitation strategies should be considered:

• intervention;
• repair of existing windows;
• partial replacement of existing windows;
• addition of a new component to existing windows; and
• complete replacement of windows.

Not only can different strategies be applied to different windows in the same building, but also several strategies can apply to a single window. It is possible, for example, to replace the existing sash, repair the sill, and add secondary glazing.

These different strategies are discussed here in detail. It should be clearly understood that most preservation agencies encourage the retention of original materials wherever possible and practicable but allow for replacement when retention is clearly impractical.

## No Intervention

Following the survey and analysis, you may find that the windows are sound, weathertight, and in good working order and that no major work is necessary. Minor maintenance work, such as painting, caulking, or refinishing, should always be anticipated. Additional energy conservation measures may also be advantageous, such as tuning the existing heating system or adding secondary glazing or weatherstripping to the windows.

### Repairing Existing Windows

If the existing windows are determined to be of historical or architectural significance, seriously consider repairing them. To be successful, repairs may have to be combined with other actions discussed. Repairs can often improve the performance of an old window to industry standards in a cost-effective and practicable way when one or more of the following conditions exists:

• the windows are largely intact;
• the windows contribute considerably to the building's architectural or historical significance, and the cost of replication is prohibitive;
• the frames and sash are essentially sound;
• the required materials or expertise necessary for repairs are available;
• all parts of the windows can be made to fit properly without excessive energy losses or without restricting operations;
• replacement of existing weatherstripping or installation of new weatherstripping is possible;
• replacement or installation of insulated glass or additional glazing is possible, and the window panes can be replaced, if necessary, without severely damaging the existing window sash;
• repair or installation of balances to ensure proper operation of the existing sash is possible.

### Replacing Window Components

When only a part of the window is found to be deteriorated—for example, the sash or the sills—the replacement of the part may be the most cost-effective solution, especially if other parts of the window are being repaired. The replacement of window parts has to be planned thoroughly and done with great care. The repair or replacement should not be visually obvious, nor should it unnecessarily damage parts in sound condition. The compatibility between new and old parts is extremely important. When new materials such as aluminum or vinyl cover existing wood surfaces, for example, condensation can form within or against the old window. These conditions can further accelerate deterioration. When metals or plastics are used, the separation of dissimilar materials is absolutely necessary to prevent adverse reactions between them.

The process of installing new components into existing windows should also be planned carefully from an operational point of view. This is especially important in buildings that are occupied during rehabilitation. Removing to a shop the stiles and rails of sash that must be replaced, for example, is considerably less disruptive to the occupants than replacing parts of the frame in place.

When parts of the window can be repaired, this option is preferable to replacement. Replacing components of the existing window is recommended when

- part of the window is missing;
- part of the window is severely deteriorated, but the remainder of the window is in good condition or can be repaired;
- part of the window can be replaced without adversely changing the building's appearance; or
- replacement of the part will not negatively affect the surrounding or adjacent materials.

### Adding New Components

When the windows are sound enough to be repaired, consider adding a component—for example, additional glazing, new balance mechanisms, weatherstripping, thermal quilts, shades, or shutters—to improve their performance. These components should be added when

- windows are basically sound and repairable;
- the component that improves the energy performance can be installed without damaging the existing material or distracting from its visual appearance; or
- the component will reduce or eliminate deterioration of the existing windows.

### Replacing Window Units

If the windows of the building are missing or are severely deteriorated, replacement will be necessary. Replacement may be sensible also when the energy performance of the existing window is negligible and cannot reasonably be improved. Given the importance of a building's windows to its visual appearance, extreme caution should be exercised when planning window replacement. New windows may significantly alter the building's visual appearance and architectural character as a result of a change in materials, size, configuration, or color. It is extremely important that these changes be considered carefully from every perspective. When planning a replacement, take into account the installation process, the material compatibility of the new product to the existing structure, and the visual characteristics of the new window in relation to the rest of the building. Of particular concern are those cases where not all windows will be replaced. The integration of new windows into a facade where some existing windows will be retained must be done with great care. The dissimilarities among window units may become strikingly evident and undesirable when placed side by side in a facade.

The Secretary of the Interior's Standards for Rehabilitation are explicit on the question of replacement. They state that "new materials should match the material being replaced in composition, design, color, texture, and other visual qualities." Replacement of the existing windows should be considered only when

- the energy performance of the existing window cannot be significantly improved by repair or addition of components;
- the existing window cannot be made to fit tightly in the wall because of settlement or other types of deterioration in the outside wall;
- materials or skills required to repair the window are not available or are prohibitively expensive;
- the window or substantial parts of the window are missing or are severely damaged;
- the windows are not particularly significant historically or architecturally; or
- the existing windows can be replaced with new ones that do not significantly affect the building's visual appearance or architectural character.

Establishing clear project objectives is the first step in planning a window rehabilitation project. The next is to determine the project's limits based on a comprehensive analysis of the existing physical condition of the windows, including their location and orientation within the building and their potential for performance improvement. In addition, these objectives should be weighed against applicable regulations, budget, and other building rehabilitation concerns. Success in making one's strategy work ultimately depends on what products and services are available. Chapters 3 and 4 present information on window rehabilitation products and methods.

# 3

# Maintaining, Repairing, and Retrofitting Windows

After evaluating the windows' condition, consider the possible options—maintaining, repairing, and retrofitting existing windows—within the context of the project's objectives and the window evaluation. The information in this chapter is organized according to the principle that the least modification to an existing window often yields the greatest return in meeting the project's goals. This approach is in keeping with accepted preservation practice and simple economics: the ratio of investment to return is often greater when repairing and upgrading an existing window than when replacing it.

Repairs described in this chapter include wood consolidation, steel window repairs, adjustments to hardware, and replacement of glass, sash, and frame parts. Retrofit measures, intended to upgrade the performance of an existing window, are often applied in conjunction with comprehensive repairs. These include adding weatherseals, interior or exterior storm windows, supplementary or specialty glazing layers, and devices intended to control specific aspects of the unit's immediate environment, such as shutters, shades, screens, blinds, and awnings.

## MAINTAINING WINDOWS

Window maintenance is nothing more than a set of orderly tasks—cleaning, coating, sealing, adjusting, and storing components—which, when properly managed, permit the window's continued efficient operation. The number of tasks needed to maintain the unit and the difficulty of each are factors to be weighed early on when rehabilitating windows. How difficult is it to reach the window? Does the window require seasonal removal and storage of parts? How difficult is it to perform minor repairs to the window? Are replacement parts readily available? Will maintenance require an increase in staff? The answers to each of these questions may involve added costs for the building owner.

Maintenance is best facilitated by the use of a window schedule.

**Opposite: Tools of the trade at a typical window rehabilitation site. (Richard Pieper)**

The schedule should include maintenance and repair instructions for each window part and surface.

### Cleaning

Readily available household and industrial-strength cleaners are generally used to remove dirt and soot from most parts of the window unit. The majority of these cleaners contain a solution of ammonia as the basic solvent. Avoid solutions containing high concentrations of ammonia, which may damage glazing, painting, and anodized and other metal finishes or surrounding masonry surfaces, especially if the window is washed frequently.

Access to the window surfaces to be washed is a major maintenance concern, especially on high-rise buildings. Until recently window washers often gained access to exterior surfaces by affixing themselves to washer bolts attached to the frame. In many cases these washer bolts are no longer reliable. Washing as well as other routine maintenance tasks can be accomplished for the building as a whole from a suspended scaffolding system that hangs from a building's cornice, which is raised and lowered by an electric motor. Some replacement windows are equipped with more complex hardware that allows for cleaning exterior surfaces of the sash from the interior.

### Removing Paint from Wood Windows

Older windows tend to accumulate many layers of paint. This paint is likely to interfere with the proper operation of the window and is usually visually unattractive. Over time partial peeling leaves a pitted surface that encourages moisture to collect. Excessive paint layers also obscure the shape of original molding profiles, which add definition to the window's appearance.

The extent of paint removal required depends on the condition of the paint (see the discussion of windows in residential buildings in chapter 1).

**Chalked paint** should be cleaned with a mild detergent solvent, hosed down, and allowed to dry before repainting.

**Crazed paint** should be sanded by hand or with a power sander before repainting.

**Peeling and blistering** between coats should first be analyzed as to the source. If salts or impurities have caused peeling, the defective surface should be scraped off and the underlying surface hosed off and wiped dry before repainting. If the peeling or blistering was caused by incompatibility of the paints or improper application, the defective surface should be scraped off and the underlying surface sanded to provide a better bond with the new paint.

Peeling, cracking, and alligatoring to bare wood require total removal of the defective paint followed by drying out of the wood substrate and treatment for any rotted areas before repainting (see discussion of physical problems in chapter 2).[1]

**Stripping layers of paint with a heat gun and paint scraper from a 19th-century window. (Richard Pieper)**

Paint is typically removed from wood surfaces by scraping after it has been softened with heat guns or plates or brushed with commercially available chemical stripping solvents, such as methylene chloride, toluol, or xylol. The softened paint is scraped with special scraping tools designed to not damage existing molding profiles. Another commercially available method sandwiches the paint, softened by a solvent paste, between the wood substrate and a disposable membrane. Although this method is more costly with respect to materials, it is less labor intensive than scraping.

When chemical paint removers are used, take care to protect your skin, provide adequate ventilation, and prevent spillage onto adjacent materials. These solvents can etch or otherwise damage the surrounding masonry, painted surfaces, and glazing. When a heat gun is used near glass, carefully cover the glass with aluminum foil. This measure will help reflect heat away from the glass and reduce the chances of localized overheating, which can result in the glass cracking. It is best not to use these chemicals on or directly adjacent to glass.

In most cases of complete paint removal, remove the existing sash from the frame. Pry loose the stops and parting beads as carefully as possible so that the wood does not split. Once the paint has been removed, it is important to revitalize the bare wood by rubbing it with fine-grade steel wool soaked in turpentine or mineral spirits and boiled linseed oil.

After the excess paint from the window frame and sash has been removed, it may be advisable to treat the surfaces with a protective coating. Treat wood frames and sash with a commercially available preservative, taking care that the preservative selected is compatible with the finish or paint to be applied afterward. Solutions containing copper arsenate, for example, give treated wood a greenish tone.

### Removing Paint from Steel Windows

Removing paint from steel frames and sash usually includes removing some built-up corrosion and scaling. Use a wire brush, being careful not to damage the remaining glass or other surfaces. Particular attention is required to remove rust buildup at construction joints and along the crack perimeter of the sash and frame. Because older steel windows were typically primed with lead-based paint, wear a respirator when using a wire brush. An alternative to abrading the surface, particularly when only light corrosion is present, is to use a liquid gel containing phosphoric, ammonium citrate, or oxalic acid. After the gel has been brushed on and has set, the steel substrate should be wiped clean and dried. Again, protect surrounding materials, particularly masonry and glass, during all these procedures. After removing the paint, wipe the bare metal with a solvent such as benzene or denatured alcohol to remove all chemical residue.

If corrosion is extensive, sandblasting may be necessary. Remove the sash from the frame and the glass panes from the sash. A low-pressure blast (80 to 100 pounds per square inch with small grit) applied with an easily controllable pencil blaster is recommended.

Because corrosion begins as soon as the bare metal is exposed to the air, apply a rust-inhibiting paint immediately after removing old paint. Two coats of zinc-rich chromate paint as a primer are recommended and the finish coat of paint should be from the same manufacturer as the primer to ensure compatibility.[2]

REPAINTING. The most time-consuming maintenance procedure is repainting windows. Careful surface preparation is the key to a successful job. In the case of wood windows, once the wood has been preserved and its moisture content reduced, select a paint that resists moisture but allows the wood to breathe. Steel windows should be primed with an anticorrosive primer and finished with a compatible paint.

The development of the modern coating industry has resulted in a complex array of paint options. Paints containing lead, used in the past on both wood and metal windows, are no longer readily available. Solvent- and water-based paints used today are generally thicker in composition than the solvent-based paints used historically. When selecting a paint, seek assistance from manufacturers or suppliers about compatibility and methods of application.

When selecting a paint consider these factors:

- drying and recoating time;
- coverage;
- environmental factors, such as toxicity and flammability;
- adhesion;
- color and gloss durability;
- moisture permeability (in wood windows);
- expected service life;
- compatibility with window putty;
- tolerance to adverse weather conditions; and
- adhesion between contacting surfaces.

The earliest water-based paints, now often referred to as latex, were developed for use on interior surfaces and performed poorly on exterior surfaces. For wood windows today's exterior water-based vinyl acrylic paints are generally more compatible with existing paint layers containing lead and provide better moisture permeability than water- or solvent-based alkyd paints. If the paint layer is impermeable, it may trap water that penetrates past the paint film. Alkyd paints available in flat, semigloss, and gloss finishes are fast drying, flexible, and resistant to chalking and retain color and gloss well but are incompatible with existing paint layers containing lead. A solvent-based alkyd paint rich in zinc or zinc chromate is generally recommended as a primer for steel windows along with an impermeable alkyd finish coat.

### Caulking and Glazing Compounds

Caulking and glazing compounds are used to seal a window's non-operable joints. Because their expected service life varies from 5 to 30 years when the window unit is properly maintained, they are considered a disposable part of the window unit requiring periodic maintenance. Replacing cracked or missing compounds is somewhat complicated because of the development of new materials since World War II.

Most traditional caulks and glazing compounds had a base of linseed oil, which tended to became hard and brittle over time. Today, more than a dozen generic compounds are commercially available to fill seams and joints. Most are based on more complex plastic and silicone compounds and tend to remain pliant for a longer time, but not all are useful in window rehabilitation. Because of windows' exposure to temperature extremes and the stresses that develop at the joints where dissimilar materials meet, compounds should be durable, flexible, and resilient.

CAULKING. Caulking is used to bridge the joints between the frame and the window opening. These should not be considered stationary joints, for they are constantly moving as the wall and window materials expand and contract because of changes in temperature and moisture content. Selecting an appropriate caulking also depends on the window material itself. The dimensions of a steel window within a window opening, for example, change less than a wood window does. Both, in turn, are more stable than an aluminum window, which is the most dynamic material and thus requires the most sophisticated caulking.

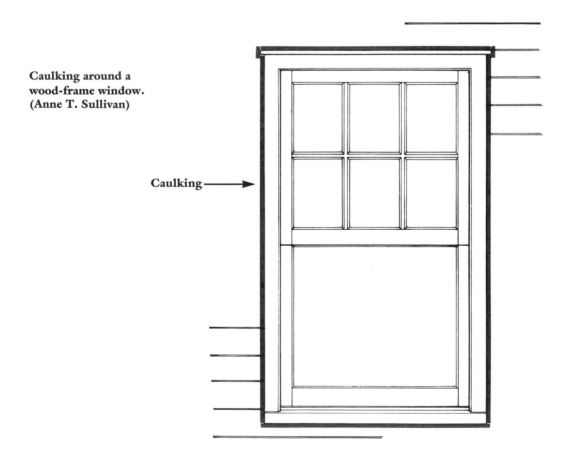

**Caulking around a wood-frame window. (Anne T. Sullivan)**

Caulking

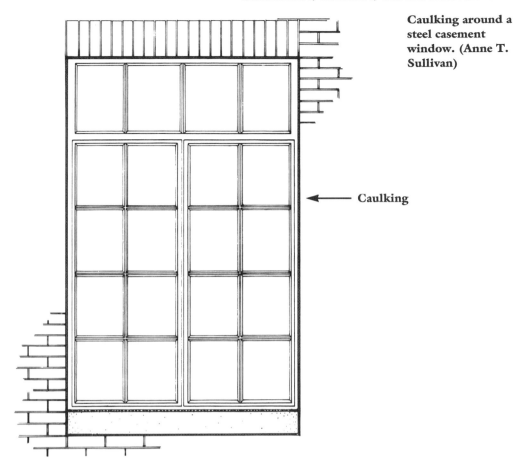

**Caulking around a steel casement window. (Anne T. Sullivan)**

← ─── Caulking

When selecting caulking be sure to consider

- the material of the window opening (some compounds do not adhere well to porous materials);
- the width of the joint to be sealed (some compounds have a limited gap range);
- the season when caulking is to be applied and the curing time (some of the better compounds require extended periods of warm temperatures above 60°F); and
- the caulking's integral color range, often available by custom order, or its adherence to paint.

Commonly used window caulks include oil-based, butyl rubber, polysulfide, and silicone compounds.

**Oil-based caulks** can seal joints of up to ½ inch and are the least expensive but can require up to a year to cure and temperatures above 40°F for application. They dry hard and can deform permanently.

**Butyl rubber caulks** can seal joints of up to ½ inch, adhere well to metal and masonry, and can be painted upon cure but require temperatures above 40°F for application. They are subject to shrinkage, and some degrade under exposure to ultraviolet light.

**Polysulfide caulks** can seal joints of up to 1 inch, are flexible and resilient, but are more expensive. They require temperatures above 60°F for application, as well as careful surface preparation and application of a primer over porous surfaces.

**Silicone caulks** can seal joints of up to 1 inch, are flexible and resilient even at low temperatures, and can be applied at temperatures as low as 0°F. They are the most expensive, have limited integral color range, cannot be painted in most cases, and require careful surface preparation and application of a primer over porous surfaces.

**Polyurethane caulks** used in some steel windows, can seal joints of up to ¾ inch, are flexible and resilient, and adhere well to masonry. They require application at temperatures above 40°F, careful surface preparation, and application of a primer over most surfaces.

When caulking a window, carefully scrape out the existing compound and residue before applying new caulking. If the joint is large and deep, provide packing directly behind the joint. Protect adjacent masonry surfaces before caulking, since some compounds stain. Review and strictly follow manufacturers' recommendations and instructions.[3]

Gaskets are used in place of caulking in more complex contemporary window types and curtain walls. Discussion of these applications is not within the scope of this manual as they usually require professional assistance.

GLAZING COMPOUNDS. Glazing compounds are used to seal the joints where the panes of glass meet the muntins and sash members in

**Oil-based glazing compounds and glazier's points secure glass in wood muntins.**

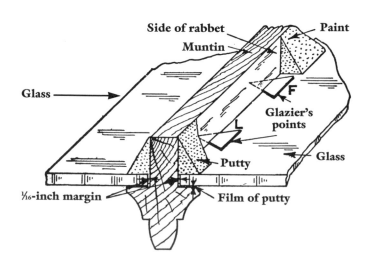

older, single-glazed windows. An oil-based putty is typically used in wood sash, while specially formulated glazing compounds are used in steel sash. Most compounds are intended to be protected by paint but harden with age and rapidly deteriorate when exposed to the elements. Sections of deteriorated glazing compound can often be replaced without removing the sash from the frame. Complete replacement of the compound, however, is best accomplished with the sash on a horizontal surface and the glass removed.

When completely replacing the glazing compound, remove all deteriorated material manually by scraping, taking care not to damage the rabbet, where the glass is positioned. If the putty or other compound has hardened in the rabbets, it can be softened by heat. Before the glass panes are replaced, the surfaces of sash members should be prepared. For wood sash clean and finish bare surfaces by rubbing the surface with a fine-grade steel wool or a fine grade of high-quality sandpaper and then apply a solution of equal parts of boiled linseed oil and turpentine; finally, prime and repaint. For steel sash remove any corrosion, prime, and repaint. For wood sash and most steel sash apply a thin bed of putty along the inside face of the rabbet. This process, known as back-puttying, provides a tight seal and protective cushion for the glass. Insert the glass, replace glazing points or clips, and putty the exterior face in a neat triangular bead. Paint the glazing compound, allowing the brush to overlap and drag slightly over the glass to form a durable seal.[4]

## REPAIRING EXISTING WINDOWS

Window repairs, such as consolidating wood sections, bending steel sections, replacing glass, adjusting hardware, or replacing damaged wood, steel, or aluminum sections, are frequently performed as needed during the course of maintaining a building. Such repairs greatly improve the performance of older windows by returning them to their original state.

Work items can be scheduled on a unit-by-unit basis when windows throughout the building are being rehabilitated. Since most repairs in an occupied building require removal of the sash from the frame, temporary enclosure of the opening is required. Undertaking a program of comprehensive repairs in an occupied building is more difficult and usually more costly than in an empty one, for it usually requires some interior access to the unit and disrupts the occupants' routine. Although repairs can be performed off site, they can be greatly expedited by establishing a shop on the premises.

### Fillers and Consolidants for Wood Windows

Repair of deteriorated wood sash and frame members is possible in cases where there has been loss of material. It should be considered a primary option when joints have not twisted or warped, as when the

Applying low-viscosity, epoxy consolidant on wood rot. (Richard Pieper)

Filling voids in deteriorated wood with epoxy filler after wood consolidation. (Richard Pieper)

surfaces of sills, lower portions of the frame, and bottom rails of sash have become eroded but have not cracked or split. Filling and consolidation of most frame members is performed in place, while sash consolidation is usually done in a shop.

When only wood surfaces are eroded, voids can be eliminated by applying a paste or putty filler. Apply fillers after the wood has dried and has been treated with a fungicide and a solution of boiled linseed oil.

In cases where a limited amount of rot has progressed well into the substrate, interior voids are filled in by saturating the wood with a penetrating epoxy consolidant formulated for wood. Surface voids as well as decayed or missing ends near joints are then filled or built up with an epoxy compound.

When sash are in such poor condition that they require consolidation, reputtying and painting are typically also needed. Moreover, the joints connecting stiles and rails are likely to have become loose. After the glass and paint in areas to be treated have been removed, the sash is placed in a jig on a horizontal surface. Separated corners should first be repaired by pulling the joints together with a pipe clamp, drilling holes through adjacent stiles and rails, and securing the joints with a blind dowel. Rotted, missing, or eroded sections are then treated with the saturating epoxy, allowed to cure, and resurfaced with the epoxy paste. Surfaces are then sanded and painted as required.[5]

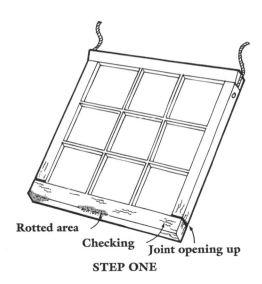

Rotted area   Checking   Joint opening up

**STEP ONE**

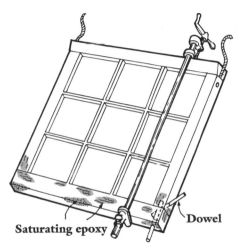

Saturating epoxy   Dowel

**STEP TWO**

Epoxy paste

**STEP THREE**

Repair of deteriorated joinery with epoxy consolidants and fillers. (Architectural Record)

### Repair of Steel Windows

Repair of steel windows usually involves special tools and is best done by skilled contractors. Among the methods they use are filling surface voids with compounds formulated for metal, straightening deformed sections by force and heat, and splicing in new metal.

Corrosion-pitted, dented, or other uneven surfaces on steel windows can be built up by applying patching compound used in automobile bodywork, plumber's epoxy, or a mixture of steel fibers mixed in an epoxy binder. Eliminating these imperfections reduces the risk of further damage from standing water, especially on horizontal surfaces.

Bent, bowed, or misaligned steel window sills and lintels can often be straightened in place by removing the glass, bracing the window with a wood support, and slowly applying pressure to bend it back into alignment. Heating the steel before applying pressure makes it

**Repairing steel windows in an apartment building from the 1930s. (John Seekircher)**

more malleable. Take care not to overheat the steel. When the metal section has been so greatly reduced by corrosion that it will break when bent, a new metal plate can be welded or tapped and screwed into the existing steel member.[6]

The presence of rust does not always indicate a structural failure, and typically represents a very small loss of material. But since the act of rusting is a process of the material expanding, rust often indicates the development of new stresses in the window opening.

### Glass

Old glass has a texture and often a color that contribute to the window's appearance. When deciding whether to replace cracked or broken glass or how to replace missing glass, first itemize the visual characteristics of the existing glass. Whenever possible, salvage the original glass. It is often possible to reinstall the remaining original glass in a limited number of windows or at the edges of the crack.

When reinstalling old glass, mark the top of the glass with tape before removing it from the sash so that it can be replaced in the rabbet in its original direction. Glass is formed from a liquid, and the longer it has been in place, the thicker it is at the bottom. Proper reorientation is of particular concern with cylinder glass, which has other uneven sections as well.

When replacing glass in an existing sash, measure both dimensions in each pane and allow a minimum of $\frac{1}{16}$ inch for expansion in the sash. For wood sash first coat the glazing rabbets with linseed oil to prevent the wood from soaking up the oil from the putty. (See chapter 2 for information on the use of glazing compounds.)

Many types of glass—replacement crown, cylinder, float, plate, wire, textured ("novelty"), colored, and stained glass—are available today as new products or in the salvage market. Replacement cylinder and crown glass and to a limited extent float glass provide some texture and sometimes tinting, but avoid contemporary forms of "antique" glass that exaggerate imperfections and are conspicuously different from the originals. Other historic types of glass, especially those originally developed and marketed for a particular purpose or produced within a limited time span, such as colored, wire, and novelty glass, are difficult to match.

Tempered and laminated glass, which were not used historically, are also available as replacements when strength or shatter-resistant properties are required. However, they require special handling and cutting, thus presenting considerable installation difficulties in multi-pane sash.

Other types of replacement glass are used to reduce the solar gain or limit ultraviolet entry. These include tinted, reflective, and heat-absorbing glass. This type of glazing is usually limited to applications where climate control is critical, such as museums or laboratories. Most of these special glazings substantially alter the window's appearance.

### Hardware

Expect to make some adjustments to the window's hardware during the course of the unit's life or during its rehabilitation. First consider the hardware's functional and decorative nature. Pulls, hinges, latches, and sash locks, like the window unit itself, tend to accumulate paint that restricts proper operation. Often, removing the paint and lubricating these parts is the least expensive way to renew hardware. Ornamental hardware is expensive to replace and should be retained whenever possible.

When the original hardware is no longer required for the window's operation, consider maintaining it in place if it will not inhibit operation. Various replacement products are available, including some stock period castings that may be appropriate to the window's style and period.

**Sash locks and latches,** which may be necessary to improve security as well as the windows' fit, are available in both reproduction and contemporary designs.

**Sash balances** include weights, pulleys, spring and pressure balances as well as modern designs for tracking mechanisms, and block-and-tackle and spring-balancing mechanisms for double-hung sash. New sash weights may be required in a window rehabilitation plan if weight is being added to the sash by an additional layer of glazing material. Lead, which is heavier than cast iron, can be substituted in cases where space is limited in the weight pockets. In windows that do not have a proper double-hung mechanism, new tracks can be installed on the window frame, improving operation as well as fit.

**Hinges** for closing, extending, or sliding windows and various types of pivot hardware, cranks, and other operating hardware are more difficult to replicate, but many contemporary designs can be installed on existing steel windows.

If possible, equip windows in the building's more important public spaces with recycled original hardware.

### Replacement Parts

When sash and frame parts cannot be repaired by consolidation, consider replacing the part while retaining other sound components, such as glass or operating hardware. This approach often involves custom work but makes sense when the deterioration follows a pattern such as repeated sill failures.

Keeping a stock of replacement parts on hand is recommended as part of standard maintenance operations after a major rehabilitation.

WOOD WINDOWS. Most replacement sash and frame parts can be obtained from local millwork shops or yards. In general, try within a reasonable cost to maintain the molding profiles and match the original species of wood. Many millwork shops can duplicate existing moldings for sash and frame pieces by cutting new knives for the

**Repair of a steel window may require welded replacement of deteriorated members. (John Seekircher)**

molding shapes. This custom work can be costly, especially if only small amounts of one or many different molding profiles are needed. Some custom millwork shops keep a selection of original or newly cut knives from other projects and will run acceptable profiles at less cost. Most millwork shops sell a selection of stock trim of similar profile and scale that can sometimes be used with satisfactory results. If the original wood species is not available for custom or stock millwork, select a wood with similar weatherability and avoid less durable species. Most installation work requires a skilled carpenter for best results.

Exterior frame elements often requiring replacement are the sill and lower sections of the frame. To replace a sill, first measure it in place, and then remove the nails where possible and cut it out. The

new sill should be made of decay-resistant wood, and its upper surface should be properly pitched away from the building to shed water. When it is not possible to nail the new sill back in place, use a nonsoluble, water-resistant glue. Replace the lower ends of the frame in a similar manner, making sure that the joint between the new and old material is smooth and watertight to prevent the migration of water into the end grain.

Most sash problems occur at the bottom rail of the lower sash or at the meeting rails of a double-hung window. Consider replacing only these elements if the remainder of the sash is sound. This work requires removing sash from the window opening to a shop and removing the glazing from the sash. When only a section of the rail is damaged, a new piece can be spliced in. In most cases, however, the entire rail or stile should be replaced, matching the original joinery at the ends.

If the stiles and rails are extensively rotted or warped but the frame is essentially sound, consider having a replacement sash made and installed. Anticipate some custom millwork; the dimensions of the window openings and sash will likely vary from today's standard sizes. Careful measuring and some planning will be required to make a tight fit. Glass salvaged from the original window can often be reused in new sash.

STEEL WINDOWS. Since the turn of the century mass-produced metal windows have been manufactured in standard shapes and sizes, some of which are still being produced today. A section similar to the one requiring replacement can sometimes be obtained from the original manufacturer or a metal supply house and spliced into the original. The other, more expensive replacement alternative is to custom roll a new steel piece and then weld or screw it into place. Generally, the replacement of complete sash is custom work executed by iron workers.

## RETROFITTING EXISTING WINDOWS

The goal of all retrofit measures is to improve the window's ability to control certain aspects of its immediate environment. Numerous products, or window "additives," are available to reduce the infiltration of air, water, and noise as well as reduce conduction and solar gains. These include weatherstripping, storm windows, coated and additional layers of glazing, shades, blinds, shutters, and films. Environmental simulation tests conducted in the field during projects involving retrofit measures indicate that existing windows can be upgraded to meet or exceed the current performance standards of replacement windows and at less cost than the cost of purchasing replacement windows.

Retrofit measures should be given serious consideration when the windows are in sufficiently sound condition and major repair work is planned. Some modifications to frame and sash parts are usually required. Adding many built-in weatherstripping or thermal glazing products, for example, entails routing or rabbeting existing sash members. Since much of the cost of retrofit is replicated in removing, handling, and reinstalling activities performed for the physical repair of sash, it makes sense to conduct retrofit and repair projects in tandem.

### Weatherstripping

Although weatherstripping is one of the least expensive components of a window, it can be responsible for as much as 50 percent of its energy performance. Weatherstripping is used to reduce air and water infiltration at the crack perimeter. It is also effective in reducing noise infiltration. Weatherstripping is found in windows subject to rehabilitation and is installed routinely in new replacement windows.

Air tends to behave like a liquid in that it will seek out even the smallest hole. When the rate of air flow is accelerated, a discontinuous seal can leak almost the same amount as an unsealed window. When using weatherstripping in an existing window, make sure that it is installed correctly, with no breaks at the corners or anywhere else around the crack perimeter.

Weatherstripping is available in surface-mounted and recessed applications. Surface-mounted strips have been the traditional way to seal existing windows since the 19th century. Originally made of metal, they are now available in a range of materials for installation in double-hung windows where the sash slides between stops or on surfaces where the sash rails meet and in casement windows on surfaces where the sash rails and stiles meet the frame or other sash.

Recessed applications systems are a relatively recent development, combining built-in weatherstripping with integral or newly added sash and frame components such as stops, sash rails and stiles, or additional moldings. Several of these combination assemblies can be inconspicuously attached to or integrated into the existing window. One system, for example, replaces the existing parting stop with a new stop equipped with a built-in weatherseal. Another adds an inconspicuous molded wood carrier mounted to the interior surface of the stop. Weatherseals can also be recessed within the existing sash by cutting a small slot, or kerf, in the rails and stiles. Concealing or integrating the weatherstripping in the existing window is more visually appealing.

Weatherseals for existing windows are divided into two basic categories—sliding (or wipe) seals and compression seals. The former work with parts subject to friction. The latter are intended for parts that uniformly sit against stationary surfaces. Select the proper sealing material on the basis of required performance characteristics and anticipated life.

THIN SPRING METAL STRIPS. Available in bronze, brass, aluminum, and galvanized and stainless steel, these strips are suited for both sliding and compression applications. The installed product is relatively inconspicuous and under typical conditions the material is durable. These strips are found tacked to the jambs of wood windows or fitted to steel windows with an integral friction fit clip.

**Typical metal weatherstripping includes interlocking metal strips as well as spring metal, which bears against closed sash.**

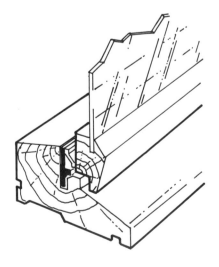

**SPRING PLASTIC STRIPS.** These are similar to spring metal. When extruded from flexible, high-impact copolymers, they can outlast and outperform conventional vinyl weatherstripping. They are applied with adhesive to the frame of metal windows. Available in colors, spring plastic will not rot, mildew, or corrode, and it conforms to surface irregularities caused by paint buildup on the mounting surface or to sash that is not plumb in the frame.

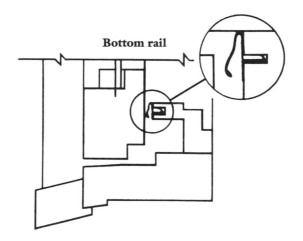

**Bottom rail**

**Spring plastic weatherstripping for double-hung and casement windows.**

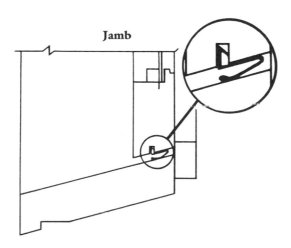

**Jamb**

PLASTIC FOAM STRIPS AND FELT STRIPS. These types of weatherseals are inexpensive but extremely limited in application. Plastic foam strips can be applied only with adhesive tape backing. Both types can be used only for compression seals, not for sliding seals. These strips are effective on metal windows with a cap of ¼ inch. Use in double-hung windows is limited to horizontal surfaces only. Both materials typically have a relatively short life span because of their porous composition, causing them to absorb moisture and deteriorate quickly. They are conspicuous when the window is open.

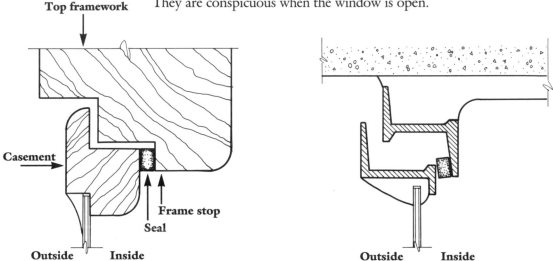

**Foam or felt weatherstripping in compression seals in wood and metal frame windows.**

ROLLED VINYL OR RUBBER GASKETS. Gaskets are extruded or molded and are generally surface mounted to the window exterior, where they are subjected to extremes of weather and ultraviolet light. The material has a life span of only several years. Also, some shrinkage and cracking—the amount depends on the specific formulation—will occur as the material ages. The gaskets can be used in either sliding or compression applications and are nailed to the sash and frame with the tubular seal portion pressed tightly against the window crack. This type of weatherstripping is also relatively conspicuous.

EXTRUDED RUBBER AND PLASTIC PROFILES. Combining a flexible lip with a rigid backing, this weatherseal is a relatively new weatherstripping material developed in Scandinavia. It combines the elasticity of natural rubber products with such characteristics of plastics as resistance to ultraviolet rays, ozone, and numerous chemicals. The rigid carrier provides a positive mounting method that can be push-fitted into a groove or kerf cut into the window frame or sash. This type of weatherstripping usually requires professional installation, but the result can be an extremely tight, unobtrusive seal.

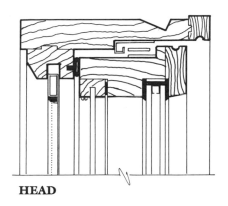

**HEAD**

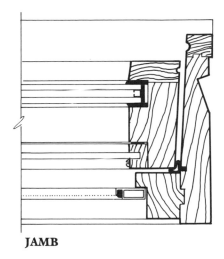

**JAMB**

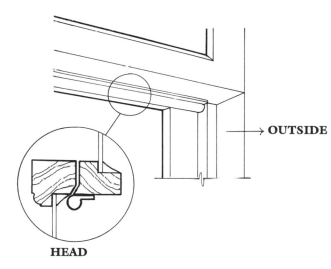

→ **OUTSIDE**

**HEAD**

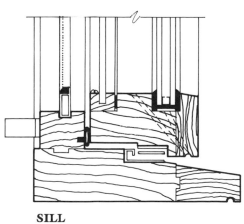

**SILL**

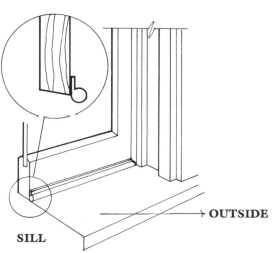

→ **OUTSIDE**

**SILL**

**Rolled vinyl or rubber gasketing is applied to the window exterior in both sliding and compression applications.**

117

FILM-CLAD FOAM. Foam is a relatively new material that works equally well as a weatherseal for both windows and doors. These foam seals are continuously molded from a flexible plastic material and clad in an ultraviolet-resistant plastic film. This product combines the durability of a closed-cell material with the soft, flexible characteristics of open-cell foam. These seals are available in a variety of profiles with a choice of fastening options, including kerf mount, adhesive, or rigid backing for channel insertion. Because of the material's resilience, it can be used for both sliding and compression seals.

**Film-clad foam stripping is durable and comes with a variety of mounting options. (3M)**

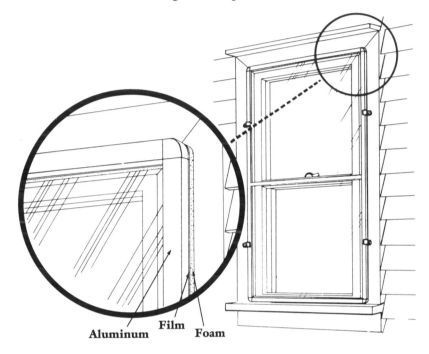

Aluminum    Film    Foam

PILE WEATHERSTRIPPING. Like that used in automobile windows, this type can be used for sliding as well as compression seals. It is made from polypropylene fibers interlaced into a supportive plastic backing. In the better seals the weatherstripping pile fiber has been treated with silicone, which repels water and reduces friction to make window operation easier.

**Polypropylene pile weatherstripping in a new aluminum window.**

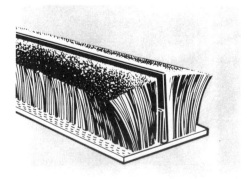 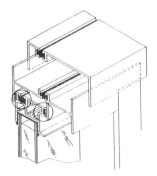

**SEALANT BEAD.** A sealant bead is an effective and relatively inconspicuous type of weatherstripping for metal windows. It entails applying a clean bead of firm-setting caulk on the primed frame and a polyethelene bond-breaker tape on the operable sash. The window is then closed until the bead has set and takes the form of the gap. The sash is then opened and the tape removed, leaving the set caulk as the weatherstripping.

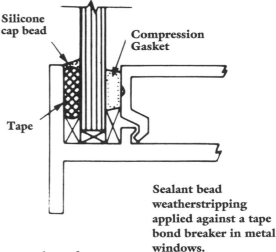

Sealant bead weatherstripping applied against a tape bond breaker in metal windows.

**COMBINATION ASSEMBLIES.** A wide range of new products has been developed in response to the requirements of building rehabilitation activity. When used properly, these combination assemblies can upgrade performance and retain the integrity of the original window structure.

When the window's original construction provides for no weatherstripping there is no space to add it without cutting into and removing the sash. As an alternative, various kinds of metal or wood carrier assemblies containing weatherstripping can be surface mounted. The most common are metal carriers, but usually these are not visually satisfactory. A better solution is to use a decorative wood molding that has a plastic T-slot embedded in it to accept a variety of rigid-backed seals. A molding shape can be selected from stock or custom milled to be compatible with the window, and the wood can be stained or painted to match the room decor.

Every double-hung wood window has a parting stop or bead that separates the two movable sash units. The parting stop is usually nailed into the frame or force-fitted (i.e., fit so tightly that it does not need nailing) and can be easily removed. A plastic replacement parting stop, which incorporates a pile or foam-clad seal on opposite sides, can be inserted into the existing slot to provide continuous contact with the sealing material as the window is operated. The visual impact of this solution is minimal. However, other measures are necessary for the meeting and bottom rails of lower sash.

Corner seals, available for sealing corners, interlocks, meeting rails, and other areas where gaps may occur in windows and doors, are generally rectangular pieces of pile, but they can also compensate for construction variations typically found in older buildings. Some of these seals can be used in combination with a replacement parting stop.

Other weather seals are available to accommodate special design conditions. These come in a variety of materials, sizes, and configurations, and at least one manufacturer will design and produce custom seals for specific applications. The cost of these special parts is surprisingly reasonable when comparing their cost effectiveness with that of a full-scale replacement program.

119

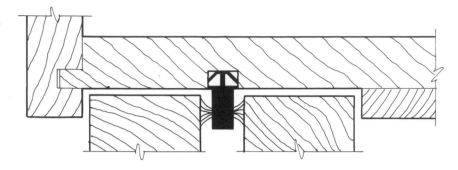

**Parting stop replaced by pile weatherstripping. (Anne T. Sullivan)**

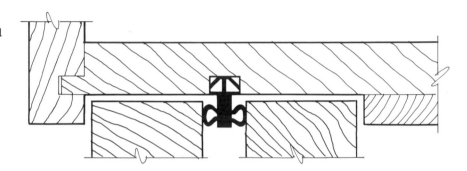

**Parting stop replaced by neoprene weatherstripping. (Anne T. Sullivan)**

### Storm Windows

A storm window added to an existing window provides an insulating layer of air, increasing the R-value of the unit and reducing noise infiltration. The deep separation between interior and exterior glass surfaces also reduces convective drafts. When the new storm windows are properly sealed, air infiltration, conduction, and radiation are also greatly reduced. The quality of the storm window selected and its installation determine the cost effectiveness of the final assembly. Storm windows are available in several materials and are designed for interior or exterior use. Exterior storm windows can have a major visual impact on a building but are often acceptable to preservation organizations because they protect the more fragile prime window and do not permanently alter the building. When considering using interior or exterior storm windows, take into account the complexity and configuration of the window shape and its panes. A multiple-glazed sash or an arch-headed window, for example, will be adversely affected by an exterior storm window.

**EXTERIOR STORM WINDOWS.** Exterior storm windows are a traditional way of shielding the existing or prime windows from the elements. If storm windows and screens are in place, evaluate their potential and consider reusing or recreating them; if they are known to have existed but are not now in place, consider installing them.

Exterior storm windows are available in a number of stock wood and aluminum models that align with the existing window's configuration. They can also be custom made to match the existing windows' detail and configuration. Hinging the storm sash at its side and using a removable screen or glazing system is one successful solution.

The visual impact can be minimized by taking into account several design factors. The storm sash meeting rail, for example, should align with that of the prime sash. The size and color of the storm sash should be sympathetic with the window frame and surround.

Most of the storm windows in use today are aluminum triple-track systems, which include two sash and a wire screen on the third track. Many use thin gauges of aluminum and small frame sections and are not very substantial. Higher-quality windows with appropriate color finishes are also available. Several national window manufacturers produce attractive and efficiently designed wood storm sash that are more in keeping with the character of older windows.

**Special window openings and window shapes can be custom made. This side-hinged, arched storm window incorporates a screen insert. (Martha L. Werenfels)**

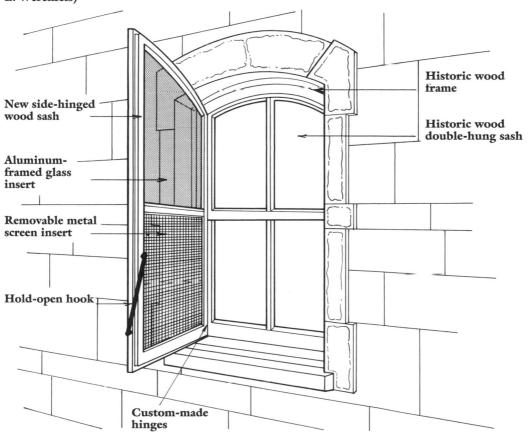

New side-hinged wood sash

Aluminum-framed glass insert

Removable metal screen insert

Hold-open hook

Custom-made hinges

Historic wood frame

Historic wood double-hung sash

**Installation of an exterior storm window in this drawing would be inappropriate because original terra-cotta ornament would be lost. (Anne T. Sullivan)**

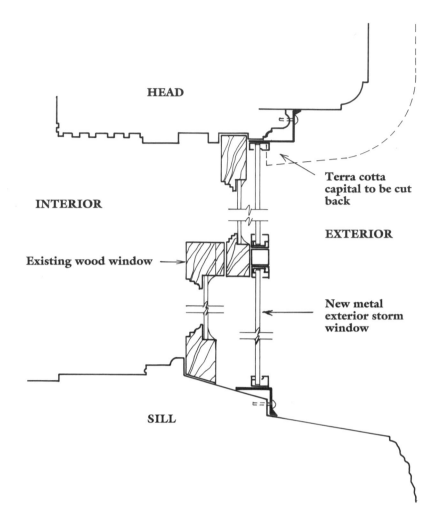

HEAD

INTERIOR

Terra cotta capital to be cut back

EXTERIOR

Existing wood window →

New metal exterior storm window

SILL

So long as the installation of an exterior storm window does not damage or obscure elements of the surround, it has the distinct advantage of preventing the destruction of otherwise easily damaged windows, an important concern in areas of extensive vandalism. When the original window system uses leaded glass, however, exterior storm windows may produce a greenhouse effect. Temperature buildup in the air space often causes the lead to buckle, especially in windows on south elevations. Venting the exterior glazing at the top and bottom will prevent this buckling, but keep in mind that this measure will also reduce the insulating value of the air layer between the glazing. In large windows using a single stationary sheet may not be possible because of weight or window pressure, and a properly designed fixed window will be required.

INTERIOR STORM WINDOWS. The installation of interior storm windows, which do not substantially alter the exterior appearance, is a more recent development and often more visually acceptable. Interior storm windows are either operable or stationary. Operable interior storm windows are basically versions of exterior storm windows but are usually made of lighter materials. Stationary interior storm windows are panels that attach to the interior frame in colder months and are removed and stored in warmer months. Since condensation collects on the unheated or exterior surface of a storm installation, in this case the prime sash, be sure to allow proper ventilation through the prime sash. Provide vents or weep holes and do not extensively weatherstrip the prime sash when using tight interior storm windows.

The prime sash's type of operation is a determining factor in the decision to use interior storm windows. Most stock storm windows are double-hung systems not intended for use with casement, hopper, or vertical or horizontal pivot windows. Although exterior sliding storm windows for in-swinging casements and interior storm windows for out-swinging casements are available, make sure that they do not obstruct the hardware and operation of the prime windows intended to remain operable year-round. If operational problems cannot be solved,

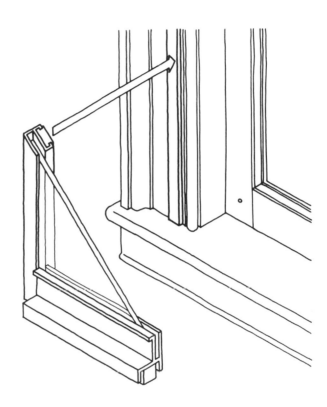

**This interior storm window has acrylic glazing set in a plastic frame. Frames are adhered to existing window trim with a magnetic seal. (Christina Henry)**

consider installing an additional layer of glazing against the existing sash (see chapter 2).

Fixed-frame glazing is available in rigid acrylic, rigid polystyrene, and polycarbonate carried in several different polyvinylchloride or metal sealing products. Typically, the frame of the interior storm window is permanently affixed to the window frame and attached to the glazing sheet by an easily removable seal that is nonetheless tight when the glazing is in place. Seals are formed by flexible polyvinylchloride retainer seals, hook-and-loop or Velcro seals, and channel and spline seals. By applying an adhesive-backed steel strip to the interior frame, storm panels can be successfully attached in a "piggy-back" arrangement.

Plastic glazing, too, should be considered for its visual characteristics and durability. Some plastic glazing may at first appear more blue than regular glass, while some has a tendency to yellow under ultraviolet light exposure. Although most plastic glazing is scratch resistant, it is not scratch proof. Local building and fire codes often have restrictions regarding the use of this material as well as fixed interior storm windows.

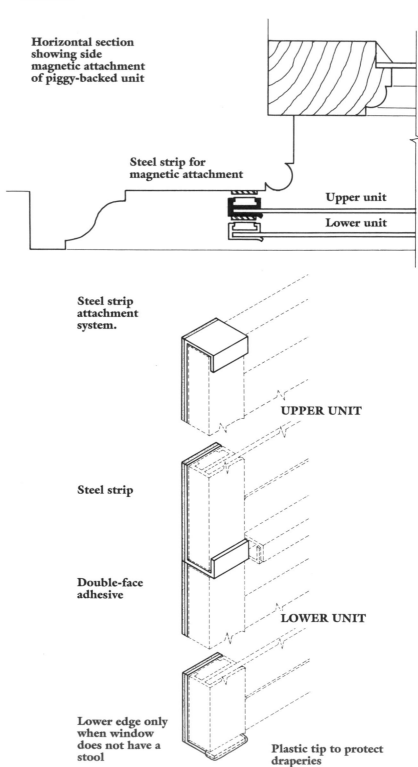

**Horizontal section showing side magnetic attachment of piggy-backed unit**

**Steel strip for magnetic attachment**

**Upper unit**

**Lower unit**

**Steel strip attachment system.**

**UPPER UNIT**

**Steel strip**

**Double-face adhesive**

**LOWER UNIT**

**Lower edge only when window does not have a stool**

**Plastic tip to protect draperies**

The addition of a steel strip to the frame of the upper portion of this magnetically adhered, fixed-frame storm window allows the lower unit to be "piggy backed" against the upper unit for storage. (Christina Henry)

## Additional Sash Glazing

Changes made to the sash glazing alone often yield positive insulating results, especially when a satisfactory weatherseal is provided at the crack perimeter. Installing additional sash glazing as well as weatherstripping at the crack perimeter and routine caulking of the exterior frame can substantially upgrade a window's energy and acoustic performance.

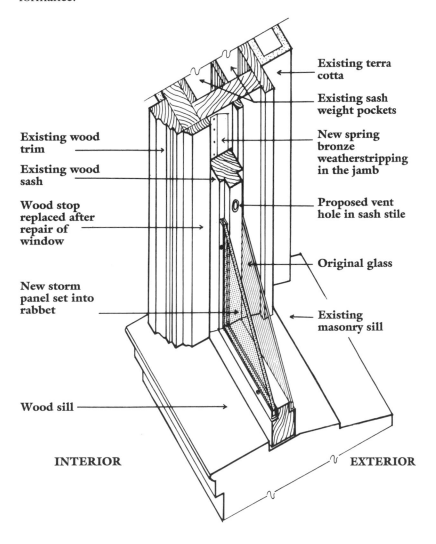

Existing terra cotta

Existing sash weight pockets

Existing wood trim

Existing wood sash

New spring bronze weatherstripping in the jamb

Wood stop replaced after repair of window

Proposed vent hole in sash stile

Original glass

New storm panel set into rabbet

Existing masonry sill

Wood sill

INTERIOR     EXTERIOR

A recessed storm panel is retrofitted by routing a rabbet on the inside of an existing sash. (Sharon C. Park)

Additional sash glazing serves to increase the window unit's R-value. Two types of additional sash glazing are available. One solution is to affix secondary glass to recesses introduced into the sash members to form an air space with the existing window pane or panes. Another solution is to use insulating glass, consisting of two or three sheets of glass enclosing a hermetically sealed air space that replaces the existing pane or panes of glass. Consider installing additional sash glazing when the window's operation or appearance would be adversely affect-

125

ed by interior or exterior storm windows. This solution is most cost effective for one-over-one sash divisions, among others.

Sealing secondary sash glazing is similar to sealing interior fixed storm glazing. The glazing is mounted against the sash using neoprene gaskets, track mounted in plastic or metal channel frames or attached with magnetic or Velcro strips. Plastic glazing can be used to reduce the weight of the sash. As in the case of fixed-frame glazing, provide sufficient ventilation to prevent fogging and condensation between the two glazing layers.

In some cases fixing the glazing directly against the sash has several advantages over interior storm windows in some applications. It provides a means of operating casement, pivot, and hopper sash in the winter. Secondary sash glazing does not work with double-hung sash unless it is fixed on sash faces that do not meet or is recessed behind the interior plane of the upper sash. Assuring a satisfactory seal usually requires introducing a rabbet along molded stiles, rails, and, where present, muntins. If plastic glazing is used, the weight of the sash will not be sufficiently increased to require complete replacement of hinges or balance hardware, although some reinforcement may be necessary.

Adding a layer of glass or plastic reduces conductive heat loss by creating an insulating double-glazed unit. This improvement is substantial compared with single glazing but not as great as adding factory-sealed insulating glass, since it requires some ventilation to prevent condensation.

Replacing the existing glass, with factory-sealed insulating glass, also known as Thermopane, Twindow, and Twinpane, can be accomplished with satisfactory results in all types of sash but is not without limitations. Existing rails, stiles, and muntins must have sufficient depth—in general, a minimum of 1½ inches—to accommodate the increased glass thickness, provide an adequate air space, hide the insulating glass spacer, and accommodate the added weight. One European approach that has been tried in this country involves remov-

**An interior storm panel is screwed into the recess of a wood sash. A neoprene gasket provides an air seal between the storm panel and the sash. (Michael J. Devonshire, adapted from a drawing by Sharon C. Park)**

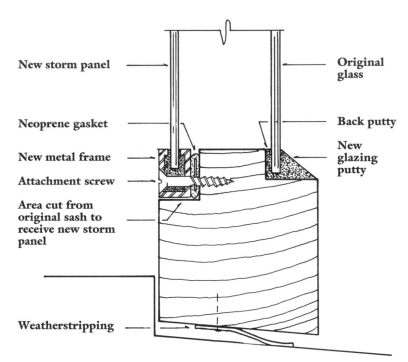

New storm panel

Neoprene gasket

New metal frame

Attachment screw

Area cut from original sash to receive new storm panel

Weatherstripping

Original glass

Back putty

New glazing putty

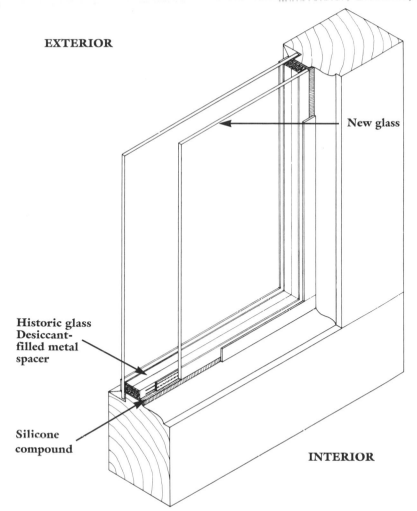

EXTERIOR

New glass

Historic glass
Desiccant-
filled metal
spacer

Silicone
compound

INTERIOR

**Innovative technology converts a standard sash into an insulating unit by sealing a second glass to the frame. A desiccant-filled metal spacer with a butyl sealer serves to space and adhere the two panels. (Christina Henry)**

ing the sash to a shop and sealing a second layer of glass to the frame without removing the existing glass. Satisfactory results have also been obtained in windows where the muntin bars have been 1 to 1¼ inches deep by using sheets of ⅛ inch glass and reducing the size of the air space. In addition, counterbalances in double-hung sash must be increased to accept the additional weight.

Although insulating glass is more energy efficient than secondary sash glazing, it is most efficient when the dimension of the air space approaches one inch. Installation is more costly because it requires removing of the sash to a shop, removing the existing glazing, and routing out sash elements to provide the deepened rabbets. In some cases installing thin metal strips inside the rabbets will reinforce the sash. Closely follow the manufacturer's installation instructions because some oil-based glazing compounds deteriorate the seals of insulating glass. Although providing ventilation is not necessary, sealed units may develop condensation over time when their seals break down; replacement is then necessary.

### Shutters, Shades, Screens, Awnings, and Blinds

Shutters, shades, screens, awnings, and blinds have been used historically to control certain aspects of the window's immediate environment. Insulating shutters and shades are used to increase the R-value of a window opening and to a certain degree insulate the opening from noise. Louvered shutters, roll-up shades and screens, awnings, and blinds reduce solar gains by shading the window opening. Although the principles on which they operate are similar to their predecessors', today's add-on components are generally more sophisticated and in the cases of shades, screens, and blinds are available as exterior products.

Two factors should be considered when selecting one of these components. Nearly all reduce the direct glare but in doing so also reduce the amount of light admitted inside. Often the most efficient measures, particularly those that reduce heat loss from the inside, have little or no transparency. The better components provide the best insulation but preclude ventilation, which may be necessary to prevent condensation.

SHUTTERS. The use of exterior and interior shutters to provide security, privacy, and shading and reduce drafts extends back to the earliest buildings in this country, although shutters have not been used continuously throughout American history. They have been subject to much experimentation, made in solid forms in some periods, and equipped with operable louvers during other periods.[7]

Traditional wood exterior shutters are still available but largely on a custom basis. Maintaining the small working parts of exterior shutters has always been difficult. Nonoperable aluminum and vinyl shutters are also available in a limited color range but are not considered appropriate in most cases.[8]

Traditional interior wood shutters also are still available from stock and custom sources. Stock units are not always easily adapted to existing window openings and rarely fold neatly into the window recesses. The insulating qualities of traditional interior and exterior shutters are negligible, although they are a conveniently operated shading source on hot summer days.

A new generation of closed-panel shutters has been developed, available with single, bifold, or quatrofold leaves. Folding panels are too thick to fold into existing shutter pockets where present and are generally mounted outside the window opening itself. The construction of most panels consists of a rigid insulation board with a high R-value sandwiched between hardboard panels finished with wood veneer, fabric, reflective foil, or a combination of these. Wood veneer and fabric finish are used primarily inside, while the foil or highly reflective finish is applied on the outside.

Insulating shutters provide a relatively inexpensive and reversible way to reduce cooling and heating loads, especially in residences that

are unoccupied during the day. A substantial reduction in solar heat gain is obtained when highly reflective finishes are used. In addition, if the closure around the shutter is tight where it meets the frame, little or no heat is transmitted by convection; thus, the amount of heat loss from the inside is also minimal. If shut tight, these shutters close out all natural daylight and require increased use of artificial light.

SHADES AND SCREENS. Interior roll-up shades also have long been used to reduce solar heat gain. Manually operated shades made of fabric or plastic are readily available. In addition to this traditional type, two newer types mounted on the interior and rolled up when not in use have emerged in the last decade: solar-control films and insulated shades.

Roll-up window shades with reflective solar-control film laminates or sunscreens provide benefits similar to solar-control films mounted directly against the glass. Because the shade is retractable, however, this solution is more adaptable than the fixed mountings on glass. Shading coefficients as low as 0.13 may be achieved. As with other shades that are tightly mounted in the frame, an additional insulating air space is established.

Two types of insulated shades are available. A window quilt or blanket consists of a heat-resistant reflective barrier such as mylar, covered on either side by polyester fiberfill or another insulation material and enclosed within a sealed fabric cover. Another type is made up of vinyl and fiberglass sheets sandwiching a dead-air space and covered

**Window quilts provide effective insulation but are bulky when rolled up and reduce natural light. (TJ Associates)**

with reflective coatings to reduce heat transfer. In both types the shades are retractable above the window opening and run in a track along the window frame to obtain maximum closure when drawn. As a result, little or no air circulation occurs between the glass and the shade. Insulating shades are more bulky than solar-reflective shades when rolled up, but they also perform far more efficiently. The shades are available in various fabric colors and patterns to be more compatible with other interior finishes. Most shades are flame retardant and can be operated manually or mechanically. As do insulating shutters, these shades reduce natural light admitted to the interior.

Little data exist about the payback of insulating shades. The shades provide a relatively high R-value and when properly installed help reduce the cooling load from 50 to 70 percent and the heat loss by as much as 45 percent.[9]

Exterior-mounted shades and screens that retract into surface-mounted housing are also available, primarily for reducing solar gains, but are not considered appropriate.

AWNINGS. Awnings, have been used on buildings since the late 19th-century to shade window openings and are still available in fixed and retractable models. Awnings provide a good shading coefficient and reduce glare without obstructing the view or substantially affecting light entry. Claims for energy savings vary, but some awnings are able to block 70 to 80 percent of the solar heat, reducing room temperatures by 8° to 15°F and providing energy savings of up to 25 percent.

Fixed awnings, which come in various shapes, consist of a fabric mounted on a tubular frame attached to the building. Although these are less expensive than retractable awnings, they cannot be adjusted to particular seasonal or daily conditions. Retractable awnings consist of a fabric awning that is folded or rolled up by a manual or motorized crank, allowing it to be used only when necessary. The fabric and mechanisms are generally concealed in large metal boxes or underneath covers that are themselves highly visible.

Awning fabrics include treated cotton duck or artificial fiber materials. Some fabrics are both water and ultraviolet resistant and flame retardant. Standard colors are available, and variations, combinations of colors, and special designs can be obtained at additional cost. The life span of the fabric is usually five to eight years.

BLINDS. The most commonly used solar-control device is the venetian blind. Blinds, originally of wood, are available today with wood, aluminum, or plastic slats that are adjustable to control the admission of light. Solar control can be further enhanced by heat-reflective surfaces. Blinds are so popular that they can be custom fit to the dimensions of specific openings and are available in a wide range of colors.

In addition to traditional venetian blinds, vertically mounted blinds, which operate in horizontal tracks, and pleated blinds are

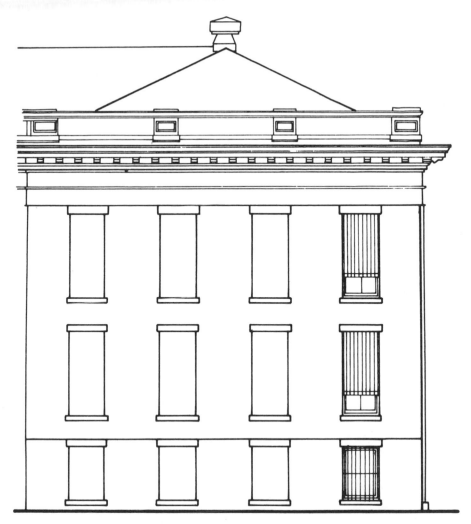

**Awnings were successfully used to reduce solar heat gain in late 19th-century buildings. (Shepard Associates, Architects and Planners)**

available. Exterior blinds are also available, but like exterior-mounted shades and screens they are not considered appropriate.

Old windows, even when in poor condition, can be successfully revitalized by establishing a program of careful maintenance and repair. Subsequently, old windows can be successfully upgraded in many cases to meet or exceed the performance standards established for today's replacement windows. In general, retrofitting a window is less costly than replacing it. The availability of skilled labor to perform the more specialized tasks described is more often than not a key determining factor in the quality of the work.

Repairs and retrofit measures are not possible in all cases. Windows, like other parts of the building, will reach the end of their service life at some time, necessitating more costly replacement.

# 4

# REPLACING WINDOWS

An overwhelming selection of wood, steel, aluminum, and vinyl replacement windows is available on the market today. Unfortunately, no one product is best in all instances. Each window type has inherent benefits and drawbacks when compared to the others. Moreover, options, quality, and cost vary among products within each generic type.

This chapter is intended to help identify through a series of questions what to look for in a replacement window and what to expect of it initially and over the long term. The field is limited somewhat when dealing with the requirements of landmark buildings, where visual characteristics are of great importance. It is not the authors' objective to recommend one product over another.

In the case of replacement windows installing a cheap unit makes no sense. A low first cost (the cost of buying and installing the unit) is nearly always offset by an ever-increasing subsequent cost of maintaining, repairing, and ultimately replacing the replacement. Manufacturers and installers will often provide on request a simple analysis of the first cost and projected payback with respect to energy savings. Such an analysis should be based on field tests conducted on site (see chapter 1) to determine energy savings through the existing openings equipped with the replacement windows.

Energy savings are only part of the payback formula. If a unit is poorly designed, built, or installed, any anticipated energy savings will quickly evaporate. Proper design, construction, and installation are factors that usually increase the unit's initial cost but greatly reduce its subsequent operating, maintenance, and repair costs.

Like all other building components, a window has five stages in its life cycle: design, construction, installation, operation and maintenance, and ultimately replacement. Problems arising in any of the first four stages will reduce a window's insulating capabilities. How well a window performs in each of these stages depends to a great degree on initial design decisions, of which the selection of material is very important.

**Opposite: Workers installing new double-glazed sash into a restored frame and jamb. (Richard Pieper)**

## DESIGN

As a machine, the window has come a long way in the last century. Today, more is scientifically understood than ever before about the actual performance of windows as insulators between interior and exterior environments. Since the 1940s the replacement window industry has made measurable improvements in the engineering of windows to reduce the kinds of problems discussed in chapter 1. Design standards for replacement windows are based on the results of laboratory simulation of environmental forces and are continuing to change as new discoveries are made.

The material the window is made of is the most important factor in its design. In addition to material selection, which is examined in greater detail later in this chapter, the design phase establishes performance standards. Performance standards for air infiltration, water penetration, wind loading, and conductivity are developed by the manufacturing industries. Attempting to meet these standards has a great impact on the window design, especially the design of component details.

Most of the window's visual characteristics—such as the shape, dimensions and proportions of structural sash and frame members, subdivision of glazing, trim, color, and finish—are also determined in the design stage.

### Performance Standards

Does the replacement window meet performance standards established by the manufacturing industry?

Performance standards developed by the industry are applied to product design on a voluntary basis. Standards differ depending on what material the window is made of. Standards are established by the National Woodwork Manufacturers Association (NWMA), the Steel Window Institute (SWI), the American Architectural Manufacturers Association (AAMA; formerly the Architectural Aluminum Manufacturing Association), the Aluminum Association (AA), and the American National Standards Institute (ANSI).

Performance standards are based on how well products perform when subjected to simulated environmental conditions in a laboratory. Laboratory tests used in the development of industry standards are conducted according to methods delineated by the American Society for Testing and Materials (ASTM) or in the case of steel windows the National Association of Architectural Metal Manufacturers (NAAMM). Systematic testing in this manner has made the design of window units more efficient with regard to specific performance characteristics.

Performance tests are typically conducted for air infiltration, water penetration, wind loading, thermal transmittance (U-value), and condensation resistance (CRF).[1] In addition, other standards are sometimes given for weatherstripping, hardware, and finishes. Such tests, originally developed for the design of windows used in new construction, have certain limitations when applied to replacement windows.

134

Lab testing indicates only performance under ideal conditions. The tested unit is typically set in a plumb and square opening with exacting tolerances, which are precisely controlled conditions more likely to be encountered in new construction than in existing buildings where the opening typically changes shape from settlement or deformation of adjacent building components.

Industry standards should not be thought of in absolute terms but as indicators of potential performance. Moreover, standards represent only minimum requirements so as not to exclude the majority of windows made of the respective material. Some products exceed industry standards, while many do not meet the minimum requirements.

Each manufacturing industry applies standards on a graded scale according to its system of subclassifying products. The lower grades, primarily intended for residential use, are designed to meet lower performance standards than units intended for commercial use. Class B wood and residential-grade steel and aluminum represent the bottom of the scale. Class A wood, heavy and standard intermediate-grade steel, and commercial-grade aluminum are designed to meet higher performance standards. Heavy custom-grade steel, and monumental-grade aluminum are additional classifications used for very large windows or windows in high-rise buildings.

Standards for air infiltration, water penetration, wind loading, and deflection are roughly comparable among wood, steel, and aluminum for residential- and commercial-grade windows. The vinyl industry does not have its own standards but has adapted those of the AAMA in some cases. The AAMA's performance standards are the highest for better-grade windows. Most manufacturers quote compliance with such standards but only those comprehensively tested by an independent lab are allowed to carry the industry seal.

Standards relating to energy and structural performance affect the window's visual characteristics, especially in the sizing of sash and frame members.

## Operation

Does the original window operation suit your needs?

Changes in a window's operation can be made without substantially altering its appearance, at least when the window is closed. It is possible to replace double-hung sash, for example, with single-hung sash, two-awning sash, or a pivot sash, if required.

Window operation is often altered to allow for cleaning sash from the interior or by hardware that allows the sash to be easily removed from the stops.

## Shape

How well does the replacement window unit fit within the existing opening?

This question is answered in large part by how flexible the unit's construction process is. Many stock units sold as replacement windows are designed according to a limited range of predetermined sizes made up of modular parts. Existing window openings rarely conform to these modules. For the unit to accommodate such modular design, the size of the opening must be reduced by installing fill panels or panning trim pieces. This change substantially alters the windows' appearance and usually results in a reduction in the unit's potential performance.

Another concern is the location of the replacement unit in the existing opening. Placing it too far in front or behind the line of the existing window changes the overall appearance. Forward placement also lends a far more substantial appearance to the sash and frame members.

Several leading manufacturers that design windows from stock parts are more flexible in sizing and locating the unit properly within the opening. Replicating windows in openings with arched heads or other unusual shapes usually requires some custom construction at additional first cost. An appropriate fit, however, pays for itself in energy performance and in maintaining the property's value.

## Dimensions and Proportions

Can the original design and detail be replicated in the replacement window? If not, how closely does the replacement unit replicate the original, particularly in terms of the sight line?

Replication can almost always be precisely done as custom work in the same materials as the original in-kind replacement at greater first cost. Some aluminum units can accept specially extruded or bent profiles, but most aluminum replacement windows have only standard panning trim. Nonetheless, these questions present the greatest challenge in window replacement projects depending on the material to be used. Many less expensive stock replacement units, once installed, simply do not look like the windows they are replacing.

**Most stock replacement window units (especially metal ones) have heavier sash and frame members than original windows, altering architectural "sight lines." (Richard Pieper)**

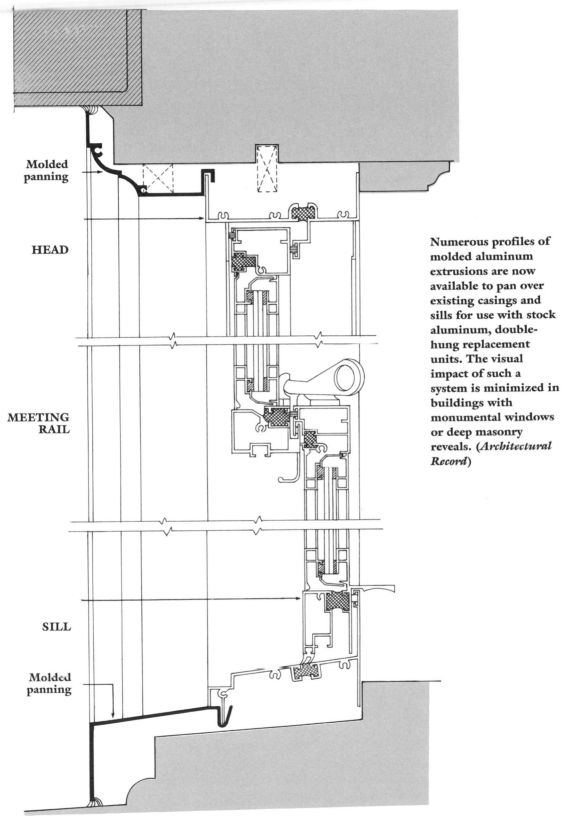

**Molded panning**

**HEAD**

**MEETING RAIL**

**SILL**

**Molded panning**

Numerous profiles of molded aluminum extrusions are now available to pan over existing casings and sills for use with stock aluminum, double-hung replacement units. The visual impact of such a system is minimized in buildings with monumental windows or deep masonry reveals. (*Architectural Record*)

"Sight line" is the term used by the industry to describe the relative proportion of glazed area to sash and frame members. Most units designed to meet industry standards contain heavier members than those used traditionally. Wood windows often require minor added mass to carry insulating glass. Metal windows, which are poor insulators, require greater added mass for the introduction of thermal breaks. Vinyl units require added mass for structural support.

Replacement units designed to be installed over existing frames, as in the case of many aluminum replacement units, result in an additional increase in the size of the members. These changes visually affect shadow lines and the architectural articulation of the various window parts.

### Glazing Subdivision

Does the replacement unit replicate the glazing division of the original?

Again, exact replication is almost always possible by custom design of in-kind replacement. Exact duplication is more difficult with replacement windows that conform to industry standards or are built of stock parts.

Replacement units are available with structural and nonstructural muntins. The former are preferable, both structurally and visually. When equipped with insulating glass, exact replication of the muntin profile is limited to windows originally containing larger muntins, because an increase in the width and depth of the muntins and in the depth of the sash is required. Structural metal muntins require thermal breaks. Nonstructural muntins are available as applied interior, exterior, or combination grids.

Nonstructural muntin systems, which do not hold glass, imitate genuine muntin configurations but may not be successful visually. (*Architectural Record*)

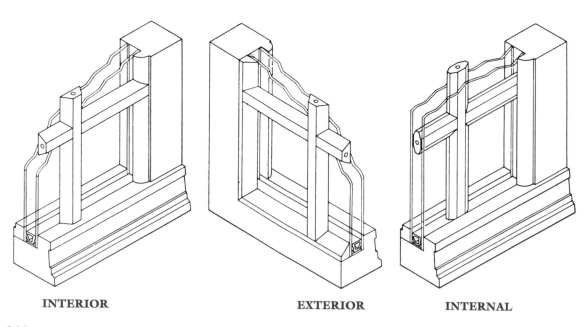

INTERIOR        EXTERIOR        INTERNAL

138

### Trim

Is the replacement unit compatible with interior decorative finishes?

Interior trim is used to cover the joint where the window meets the wall, especially in the case of stock units. Interior wood trim with molded profiles is obtainable in stock profiles that blend with original details. Such moldings are not as readily available as stock trim in other materials.

### Color and finish

What colors are available, and how will they hold up?

The availability of colors and finishes depends on the nature of the material used. Wood windows, when delivered to the site unfinished or primed, offer the widest range of colors using exterior-grade paints applied in the field. Unfinished windows can also be treated with an opaque stain. Factory-applied finishes include urethane coatings, usually available in lighter colors, as well as vinyl and aluminum claddings.

Metal finishes include baked-enamel paints and Kynar polyvinylidene-fluoride (PVF). Units with baked-enamel finishes must be shipped to the job site with great care to prevent chipping. Anodized finishing, which is a form of corrosion, is the most durable aluminum finish but limited in color range. Steel windows also can be delivered to the site primed and ready for field painting.

## CONSTRUCTION

How the window is built is determined also by the selection of material. But other factors, some already mentioned, come into play at this stage. Choosing between stock or custom construction determines the accuracy of the replication as well as the cost. How well the unit is put together has even greater cost implications in the long run. Product testing at this stage, both in the laboratory and in sample on-site installations, provides a more accurate means of predicting the unit's performance.

### Stock or Custom Construction

How do stock and custom units compare?

Most window units were based on stock items when the replacement window market developed in the mid-1970s. Increased demand and competition in the marketplace has resulted in a shift in the industry toward integrating custom features, such as sizing and shapes. Today there are two kinds of stock windows: (1) those built of modular parts to predetermined sizes and (2) those built of standard parts, sections, and extrusions that are adaptable to the size of the opening. The latter type is better suited for use in existing buildings.

Both custom and stock units have advantages and disadvantages.[2] One advantage of a stock unit is its availability in a generally shorter time, especially in the case of residential-grade units. No complex field measuring is required beyond that of the rough opening. The unit's first cost is usually less, and its design as a whole is more likely to conform to industry standards. When carefully selected, a stock window can be visually satisfactory. Some national manufacturers will further customize the unit by shaping or extruding replicated molding profiles. Replicating other visual features, such as balance mechanisms and operating hardware, however, may not be possible at a reasonable cost.

Custom construction by a smaller woodworking shop is nearly always required to match exactly an existing condition. Detailed shop drawings are needed for satisfactory custom work. Smaller shops are more flexible in cutting knives or extrusion dies for custom work or in substituting species and hardware to meet special conditions. Although the first cost is usually greater in custom work, the visual results are usually far more accurate. The drawbacks of custom work are a generally longer lead time and unknown insulating performance when the unit is not tested.

### Construction Details

How well is the window made?

In addition to minimum performance standards set by the industry, the overall performance and long-term durability of a replacement unit depends on how the unit is constructed. Joinery, material thickness, and detailing are all factors.

Joinery is important in both wood and metal windows. Wood joints should be interlocking, either mortise-and-tenon construction or finger jointing. Joints should not depend on staples or nails for tightness because these corrode and loosen over time. Surface planes of adjoining sash and frame stiles should be flush and tightly butted, with all end grain protected from exposure.

Joints in metal windows also should be clean, tight, and flush. If not, the material is not being used to its full potential in attaining exacting tolerances. No bare metal resulting from sawing should be evident at the joints; this too will corrode in time and open the joint enough to reduce its insulating value. Joints covered with sealants also indicate poor craftsmanship.

Selection of a rot-resistant species or proper fungicidal treatment are essential in wood windows. Most stock windows are made of Ponderosa pine, a soft wood with little inherent resistance to decay. Surface fungicidal treatment is usually inadequate. Treatment should consist of immersion in a fungicide for a specified period so that the solution is driven into the end grain. More durable species are available through custom construction.

Reducing the conductivity of frame and sash members is of particular concern in metal replacement units. All aluminum and some steel replacement windows require a thermal break, a plastic insulator

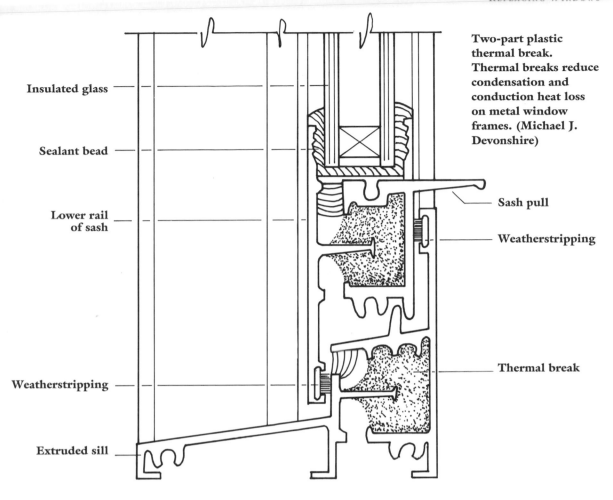

Insulated glass

Sealant bead

Lower rail of sash

Weatherstripping

Extruded sill

Two-part plastic thermal break. Thermal breaks reduce condensation and conduction heat loss on metal window frames. (Michael J. Devonshire)

Sash pull

Weatherstripping

Thermal break

between the interior and exterior sections of the metal. The most common means of introducing a thermal break in aluminum windows is to pour plastic between the two unattached sections; once it hardens, it becomes a continuous structural part of the window. In an alternative method a T-section on one extrusion is inserted into a preformed slotted plastic shape crimped into the other extrusion to reduce the risk of separating interior and exterior extrusions. Although they help overcome the conductivity of aluminum, thermal breaks that rely completely on the plastic's structural quality expose the window unit to the possibility of plastic fatigue caused by differential movement between the dissimilar materials.

The durability of operating mechanisms and hardware is also important. The quality of the balances (whether spring or block-and-tackle), sash locks, sash pulls, and cranks are good indicators of the quality of the whole window unit. The snugness and placement of sash locks as well as the quality of weatherseals serve to seal the unit.

### Product Testing

How does one know the replacement window will perform as well as expected?

One limitation of laboratory testing in the design stage is that the prototype unit tested is often carefully assembled by hand, not produced on an assembly line. Random testing by an independent laboratory of stock and custom units pulled off the line during the construction stage and field testing of a sample installation in an existing opening are two ways to provide quality control in meeting performance expectations.

## INSTALLATION

No matter how well a replacement window is designed and built, it will perform poorly if installed improperly. The extent of replacement and quality control are major factors here. A selling point of many replacement units is speed of installation (thus limiting disruption of daily activities in occupied buildings), and contractors are often paid on the basis of piecework. Some manufacturers work with select contractors and together guarantee their work. Most, however, do not, thus spreading the liability should something go wrong.

### Extent of Replacement

How do partial and complete unit replacements compare?

Replacement windows are designed to be installed in one of two ways: either as a complete unit replacement ("brick to brick") or as a partial replacement that stops short of removing the frame. The latter ranges from sash replacement, which uses the existing frame, to "no-tear-out" units that cover the existing frame, using it only for purposes of attachment.

Unit replacement involves removing all existing sash and frame parts from the rough masonry or wood opening. This is a lengthy and involved process since the frame is usually imbedded in the building's structure, and it nearly always requires additional removal of expensive interior trim. The replacement unit is then positioned, "shimmed" (i.e., wedged), and caulked in place, and interior repairs are made.

With respect to first cost partial replacement is generally less than unit replacement, for it eliminates the need to demolish the existing frame and refinish existing interior trim and finishes. Sash replacement reusing existing frames is more difficult to estimate and contract for than either unit replacement or no-tear-out systems, the costs of which are usually figured on a unit price basis. Sash replacement usually requires some repair and reworking of the frame to receive new weatherstripping; it also often requires reconfiguring of stops and balances or installation of jamb liners, resulting in minimal alteration to the window's appearance.

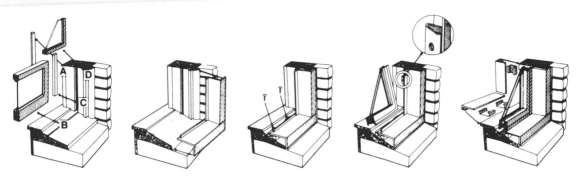

**No-tear-out installation, from left to right: removal of sash, stops, and parting strip; installation of exterior panning to cover outside frame elements; fastening of panning; installation of the window and sash unit; and installation of interior trim. (EFCO)**

No-tear-out units reduce demolition and installation time. Installing such a unit made of aluminum over a wood double-hung frame typically involves removing the sash and stops from the frame, attaching a panning frame over and to the exterior parts of the existing frame, caulking the perimeter, and then setting the new sash in place. Some units include additional extrusions placed over interior trim, while others are detailed to work with existing trim. When a no-tear-out unit is being installed over a frame considered beyond repair, additional care should be taken to provide adequate anchoring into sound substrate.

### Quality Control

How well is the window installed?

Most replacement window warranties apply to manufacturing defects, but few cover both manufacturing and installation. When there is only a single source of responsibility, there is less chance that a dispute will develop. Some window manufacturers have a nationwide network of affiliated installers who participate in product development and receive training. When a separate installer is used, be sure to obtain a clear assurance of quality and warranty regarding installation.

Performance standards should be made an integral part of the project specifications. Replacement windows are often ordered without a clear understanding of the product and its specifications. A standard of quality is difficult to establish when none was initially set. Only after the specifications are prepared and approved should installation start.

Random field testing of installed units is often used to monitor the performance standards. The owner or owner's representative selects the windows to be tested. Most reputable installers and manufacturers will readily provide and accept such testing where it has been clearly included in the project specifications. Field testing is important because the majority of window failures are due to improper installation.

## OPERATION AND MAINTENANCE

Assuming that the unit is properly installed, its operation, durability, and maintenance will determine its ultimate longevity. Every type of window has maintenance needs, both on a scheduled basis, such as replacing caulking and weatherseals, and as needs arise, such as repairing broken hardware.

### Durability

How durable will the window be?

The quality of the materials, construction, and installation of the new window will determine to a great degree the unit's durability. There are no standards governing durability because so many contingencies are involved. The window's location in the building with respect to height and exposure, the use or abuse it is subject to, and the maintenance it will or will not receive are some of these contingencies.

### Maintenance and Repairs

What kind of maintenance will the window need? How difficult will repairing the window be?

After the window is installed an important factor is its maintenance. This includes cleaning the window, keeping it caulked and adequately finished, and repairing its components as needed.

Renewing caulking is a task required in all windows. The caulking cycle will depend on the same factors discussed in chapter 2. Caulks used in wood and steel windows are generally simpler compounds and therefore easier to apply than the two-part products required for aluminum units.

Since so much of a replacement window's insulating performance depends on its weatherseals, expect to replace them during the life of the window. Weatherseals are more easily removable in some units than others. Whether they can be replaced will depend on their availability in the future.

Anodized aluminum finishes have a proven track record for being very durable over the long run. Older finishes, however, are not exempt from some surface etching due to exposure to acids and salts present in rainwater. Baked-enamel finishes promise greater durability than exterior-grade paints applied in the field, but their longevity is not presently known. A warranty of 10 years carried by some manufacturers is a general indication of industry confidence. How factory-applied finishes should be renewed if and when they fail is not clear. Expect to repaint field-treated wood and steel windows every seven years at a minimum.

Insulating glass presents another anticipated maintenance problem. As the seals fail, the glazing loses some of its insulating value, and the panes fog up. A few years ago the failure rate of insulating glass was estimated to be approximately 10 percent during the first decade of the unit's life. Improvements in seals should reduce this rate in the future, but replacement of fogged units is costly, requiring removal of the sash to a shop or, in the most severe cases, complete replacement of the sash as custom work.

Hardware adjustments and repairs also should be expected. Most balance mechanisms used in replacement windows are complex and proprietary (i.e., unique to a particular manufacturer). Parts may be difficult to procure for some. It is advisable to order spare parts at the time the windows are installed.

## REPLACEMENT OPTIONS

Each of the available types of replacement windows—wood, steel, aluminum, and vinyl—has certain strengths and drawbacks in relation to the others. This section examines some of the differences and similarities in their application and visual accuracy.

### Wood Windows

Wood windows offer great flexibility in design and detail. Because the material is easily worked, it is adaptable to custom work. Stock wood replacement windows are available for sash replacement and as both no-tear-out and unit replacements. Custom wood windows are available for sash and unit replacement.

Partial replacement is a more practical option for wood windows than for windows made of other materials. When the existing wood frame is in sound condition and requires only minor repairs, the sash can be replaced as custom work when it is exactly replicated in its single-glazed form and reuses existing sash weights and cords or stay bars. If properly detailed, weatherstripping and secondary glazing can be added directly to the sash.

The unit can also be upgraded by replacing the sash and resetting it in a jamb-liner system. After window stops and the existing sash are removed, new tracks equipped with weatherseals are applied to the jambs of the frame. These jamb liners, made of vinyl or aluminum, are essentially the same as those used in replacement window units. Once installed, the new sash is inserted, in some products backed with a foam material providing compression and a tighter seal. Sash installed in jamb liners can be tilted for easy cleaning, but the jamb liners themselves are usually highly visible.

Replicating divided sash made of light-weight wood and equipping it with insulating glass remains difficult.[3] Replicating early muntins, which typically range from an extremely delicate ⅝ inch to 1¼ inches in width, is not structurally possible when heavier and deeper glazing is used. Heavier glazing usually requires a minimum of 1½ inches to provide a sound tenon and glazing rabbet deep enough to cover the insulating glass spacer, the piece that separates the two panes

145

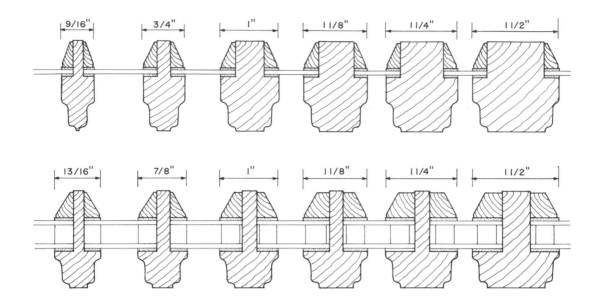

| 9/16" | 3/4" | 1" | 1 1/8" | 1 1/4" | 1 1/2" |

| 13/16" | 7/8" | 1" | 1 1/8" | 1 1/4" | 1 1/2" |

**Here the muntin width and sash thickness limit the use of double glazing in historic and reproduction sash. Muntins greater than ¾ inches wide provide sufficient space to cover the glass spacer of the glazing units. (*Architectural Record*)**

of glass of a thermal sash. Specifying an anodized bronze finish on the aluminum spacer helps reduce its reflectance.

Custom-fitted stock window systems provide a solution to this problem. The sash is equipped with a removable secondary glazing panel seated in a rabbet, thus preserving the structural integrity of the muntins. By recessing the muntins to the depth of the secondary glazing panel, sliding sash can easily pass by each other. The absence of sealing provides an adequate relief from condensation.

### Steel Windows

Steel windows, introduced at the beginning of this century, provide great strength while using relatively small cross sections for frame, sash, muntin, and mullion members.

Standard steel windows available as replacements today are generally built of rolled sections that are mitered and welded together. Hardware and hinges are usually made with bronze or brass sections, while the glazing beads may be of extruded aluminum alloy sections. Most depend on weatherstripping to reduce infiltration and seal the unit from moisture penetration. Pressed steel sections are sometimes used in addition to the standard rolled sections to vary the design. Pressed steel is generally used to construct panels or sections between windows, articulate vertical and horizontal members, and strengthen exceptionally large windows. Pressed elements are typically custom made.

Since many of the parts were originally made of proprietary rolled sections, sash replacement in an existing steel window can be done on a custom basis, although it is not as common an option as with wood windows. The replacement of fixed-frame sections, however, usually requires burning out the pieces and welding new sections in place. In most cases this is less costly than replacing the entire unit.

The range of substitute materials applicable to steel windows is also limited because of the thinness of the sections. Most aluminum replacement windows are too thick, although several window products being developed show some promise.[4]

Steel windows with narrow sections are not made with a thermal break and in some cases do not need one. The thermal performance of steel windows with respect to their U-value is superior to that of aluminum windows. This is partially due to steel's lower conductivity rate and the small size of the steel members that are continuously in contact between the inside and outside environments.

### Aluminum Windows

Many types of aluminum replacement windows are available. Not all are of similar quality, performance, long-term durability, or cost. The first cost is determined to a great degree by whether the unit is constructed as a custom or stock item.

Most aluminum replacement windows are manufactured of extruded aluminum sections of an alloy. The aluminum thickness depends on the unit's structural requirements but is usually not less than 0.06 or 0.065 inches, in accordance with AAMA standards. Higher-quality windows have an aluminum thickness of 0.07 to 0.08 inches, which is required for heavily loaded pieces such as the sill. The individual members of the frame and sash are connected by brazing or welding or most commonly by mechanical connections.

Aluminum replacements are either stock or custom built. While standard-size windows may have initial cost advantages, custom-fitted windows provide a better visual and physical fit. Standard-size modular units are dependent to a great degree on sheet aluminum panning, which is cut and bent to compensate for dimensional variations within the opening. The structural design for either type is not significantly different, but the way the frame is assembled with regard to panning is. Trim affixed to the frame at the plant is

The large, flat, aluminum pannings, which are sometimes used to cover window jambs and heads, can alter window sight lines dramatically. (EFCO)

generally thicker than the thin panning trim that is cut at the site. For the sheet to bend, the gauge of the aluminum trim has to be minimal, often resulting in some warping when large sections are to be used. Replacement units delivered to the site with panning in place and the mitered joints backsealed have better connections than those assembled in the field.

The visual difference between original wood windows and some aluminum replacements is apparent in large frames where the jambs and window heads are covered with large boxlike sections of panning trim. However, some manufacturers provide extruded running or cast-raised molding profiles, which replicate those used in older wood windows. This custom trim relieves the boxlike appearance, introduces

Custom arched
aluminum pannings
are available for some
segmental arched
windows. (Richard
Pieper)

greater shadow play, and does not radically alter the window's appearance. For better durability such panning assemblies too should be constructed at the plant.

Aluminum can be custom shaped exactly to the contours of an arched opening. Many available products are not flexible enough to handle such custom work, and the panning is cut around the archlike chimney flashing or used to cover the arch.

Structural muntins and mullions in aluminum windows, as in wood windows, are difficult to dimension because of the thermal break. When glazing subdivisions are required to match an original design, an applied type of muntin grid system snapped or screwed in directly against the glass is usually used. To eliminate dirt collection

149

behind the grid when applied on the exterior, glaze is also commonly applied between the grid's layers of insulating glass. Glazing between layers is not a visually satisfactory solution, for the muntins are usually obscured by the reflectance of the outer glass and are evident only when backlighted at night.

### Vinyl Windows

The vinyl replacement window is a relatively recent development. Its construction usually consists of a number of differently shaped extruded vinyl profiles that are mitered and joined together at the corners. In this respect it is similar in technology to the design and manufacture of aluminum replacement windows. A galvanized steel section, fully concealed inside the unit, is sometimes incorporated into the construction of a vinyl window when additional strength or stiffness is required.

Extruded sections of vinyl windows are strong, lightweight, and resistant to rot and do not require painting. As a result, maintenance requirements are likely to be limited. The materials are not susceptible to moisture, and their dimensional stability is not affected by water. Heat-cured acrylic finishes applied to the material after completion of the extrusion are considered scratch resistant but are quite brittle and once damaged are not easily repaired. Standard finish coatings come in a limited range of shades, but special colors are available for large orders. A major advantage over aluminum may be the fact that the material does not rely on a protective coating.

Extruded vinyl windows generally come as stock items with standard dimensions but are custom sized for each application. When specially shaped units and molding profiles are available, cutting special dies is costly and done only in special circumstances and for large orders.

Vinyl units are available for no-tear-out applications, allowing installation over the existing frame after the stops have been removed. The new sections are secured to the old frame, and standard panning trim is clipped on or secured by screws to the existing wood. In some instances the new unit is placed in front of the existing window system, and the remainder of the frame is covered by trim, thus substantially changing the window's appearance. Because of rigid standardization of components, differences in size have to be accommodated by standard sizes expanded with panning trim. Because the material cannot easily be worked with in the field, adjustment is limited. Exterior molded trim is not yet available.

Vinyl windows do not require a thermal break because the material has relatively low conductivity. As a result, the radiation inside the unit is lower than with aluminum replacement systems, resulting in a substantially better condensation resistance factor.

As a window replacement unit for landmark applications, the vinyl extruded unit seems to offer only limited possibilities, although it is competitive in price with aluminum. It cannot yet match the visual design characteristics of older windows, and colors are limited. Moreover, the long-term durability of plastics has to be seriously questioned.

A window's efficiency is defined in terms of its overall performance during the course of its lifetime. Some but by no means all of these performance characteristics—especially those relating to energy, structural strength, and moisture protection—are measurable by laboratory tests. Others equally important, such as long-term durability and maintenance, are subject to a complex range of factors. A good question to ask before replacing a window is, Should the new window last as long as the old window under the same conditions? If the answer is no, think again. All replacement windows are not alike.

# REHABILITATING WINDOWS IN LANDMARK BUILDINGS

Buildings designated as landmarks are fixed points in a changing world—sources of visual refreshment and temporal reference. Few features are as critical in establishing a sense of time in a landmark building as its windows. Windows reveal the subtlest of clues, from the technological limitations and aesthetic aspirations of the era during which it was built to the building's present condition. The reflectance, surface texture, and tint of window panes in old sash, the delicate thinness of weathered early 19th-century hand-planed wood muntins or exuberantly robust machined millwork of the late 19th and early 20th centuries—all contribute to a building's historic character.

A multipaned, Greek Revival casement window adds interest to the facade. (Wesley Haynes) Opposite: Window maintenance on a Greek Revival building (c. 1880) at Snug Harbor Cultural Center, Staten Island, New York. (Richard Pieper)

**Hand-blown, bull's-eye panes set in lead cames lend texture to this double-hung window. (Mark A. Weber)**

Because few features are as easy to change as windows, their rehabilitation, especially their replacement, concerns those responsible for regulating landmark buildings. Thirty percent of the surface area of an older building may comprise windows. The problem is that contemporary windows generally do not look much like their elder counterparts. Eliminating or altering a window's original glazing division or reproportioning its sash and frame members radically alters a building's appearance.

## LANDMARK AGENCIES

Landmark designation is a legal process. A building is designated either individually or as a component of a larger district. For the purpose of this discussion both shall be referred to as landmarks. Beyond this basic distinction there are essentially two kinds of landmarks: those recognized by government agencies at the federal and state levels

154

and those designated at the local level. The former group consists of buildings and districts listed in the National Register of Historic Places and, when applicable, in state registers of historic places. Local landmarks include buildings and districts designated in accordance with municipal preservation ordinances. Most state registers contain buildings and districts listed in the National Register as well as many of those recognized locally. Not all states and municipalities, however, recognize landmarks.

National landmark designation is both similar to and different from local landmark designation, and misconceptions about each abound. All landmark agencies are empowered to designate and to a varying extent regulate buildings and districts that merit preservation. Certain proposed changes to a landmark building, once so designated, are subject to review and approval. No landmark agency is empowered to mandate changes to a landmark building. The regulatory process is entirely reactive; the agency evaluates and responds to specific actions

**Panning over the arched heads of these windows obscures their original configuration and character. (Mark A. Weber)**

155

Basic repairs to the window jamb of a landmark building typically do not require a permit. (Richard Pieper)

proposed by the owner of the property in question. Most local landmark agencies use standards similar but not identical to those used by state and federal agencies as the basis for approving or denying changes to landmark buildings.

One difference between the two is the extent of regulation. State and federal regulation is more limited, triggered only when funds from state or federal sources are used to rehabilitate a building listed in the National Register or when the owner of a listed building is seeking certification for an income tax credit (ITC) under the provisions of the

1986 Tax Reform Act. When this work is reviewed, the State Historic Preservation Officer (SHPO) and the National Park Service employ the Secretary of the Interior's Standards for Rehabilitation (see page 161–64). Rehabilitation work performed on other National Register properties is not subject to regulation.

Any exterior work on buildings locally designated as landmarks, on the other hand, requires a formal review process in nearly all circumstances. In New York City, for example, approval from the Landmarks Preservation Commission, a city agency, is required before rehabilitation work on the exterior or designated interior of a landmark building begins. Some local agencies use the Secretary of the Interior's Standards, while others, including the New York City Landmarks Preservation Commission, have adapted window guidelines to assist property owners seeking approval of repair, rehabilitation, restoration, or replacement of windows in buildings that are designated as landmarks or are located within designated historic districts. Basic window maintenance, such as resecuring loose blind stops, is encouraged, however, and typically does not require a permit.

Many buildings carry both federal and local designations and require reviews by more than one landmark agency, as in the case of the rehabilitation work performed on a locally designated landmark eligible for an income tax credit.

Because of the complexity of the subject, few local agencies have hard and fast rules concerning windows. Guidelines pertaining to window rehabilitation used by the National Park Service are also included with the Secretary of the Interior's Standards.[1] In general, local regulation is strictly limited to the building's exterior unless the interior is specifically designated, while the Secretary's Standards always apply to the building as a whole. Because windows are both exterior and interior features, the guidelines of the federal and local agencies may not be the same. It is always advisable to seek the guidance of the relevant agency or agencies early in the planning stages of a rehabilitation project.

## DETERMINING SIGNIFICANCE

In their review landmark agencies consider first the significance of the existing window and its relationship to the building. Next, they evaluate the appropriateness of the proposed rehabilitation measure on those features considered significant.

A statement concerning the building's significance is usually contained in the National Register nomination, the first part of the ITC certification application, or the local designation report. To be designated a landmark, a building must possess characteristics that meet the agency's historical, cultural, or architectural criteria.

These criteria, again, vary according to the landmark agency's specific context and requirements but usually include architectural significance at the local, regional, or national level or an association with historical persons, events, institutions, social movements, or craft traditions. Buildings are also designated on the basis of their architectural quality; the result may be a determination that one period in the building's development is more important than others, especially when some detail survives. After looking at the building's significance, the agency evaluates the windows' contribution in establishing this historical and architectural character.

The National Park Service, for example, identifies a minimum of four circumstances in which it considers existing windows to be important:

1. The windows are an integral part of the building's historic fabric (they are either original or at least 50 years old), and they are considered to possess material integrity.

2. The windows are highly visible from the exterior—for example, they are located on a principal facade of an attached building, on any facade of a free-standing building when equally articulated, or on the lower floors of a high-rise building.

3. The windows contribute to an interior design scheme or are located in a significant interior space.

4. The details of the windows—muntin pattern and width, mullion profile, decorative elements (such as arched tops and brick molding), setback or reveal in relation to the wall plane, color of sash and frame, and reflective quality of glass—represent the design and technology of the building's era.[2]

Most local agencies employ criteria similar to these when evaluating the significance of existing windows. In New York City in at least one building windows containing art glass also have been considered significant because of their rarity.

If the existing windows meet one or more of these criteria, the next step is to consider repairing them and upgrading their performance if necessary. Consult the procedures described in chapters 1 and 2.

If the existing windows do not meet any of these criteria, they are generally not considered significant and can be repaired or replaced after being assessed by the landmark agency or agencies.

If an owner decides to replace existing windows considered significant, no matter what their present condition, the SHPO and National Park Service require a detailed condition survey to justify this assessment. Consult the procedures described in chapter 1. The National Park Service has denied certification of projects where windows have been replaced without adequate justification and documentation.

## REGULATIONS AND STANDARDS

The Secretary of the Interior's Standards, as mentioned earlier, are used to evaluate any proposal made to the SHPO or National Park

Service. It is important to be familiar with the Secretary's Standards. The project must meet all 10 standards, not just those that pertain to windows.

The intention behind the Secretary's Standards is to retain as much of the existing window as possible. When replacement is necessary, the design of missing elements should be based on details known to have been used in the window in the past. When accuracy is not possible because of lack of information, the design of replacement windows should be compatible with the building's design. In addition, all replacement windows should be installed in such a way that they can be removed at a future date without damaging the existing building.

The procedures contained in this manual are intended to help in determining an approach to rehabilitating windows in a historic building. They can be summarized as follows:

- Collect and review all the preliminary data necessary for understanding the window's current physical condition and one's personal objectives.
- Analyze the window's condition and performance.
- Consider all the options available.

If the window can be repaired, preservation requirements can

Recently restored decorative glass windows, originally produced by the French master René Lalique in 1909 for the former Coty Building in New York City, depict intertwined vines and tulips. (Richard Pieper)

159

easily be met as long as the following conditions are evident:

- Repair techniques that respect and replicate the qualities of the existing window, including its distinguishing features and level of craftsmanship, are used.
- Problems of energy and acoustic performance and continued window maintenance are addressed in a manner that results in the least disruption of the original window material.
- Methods of repair, especially paint removal, are carefully evaluated to prevent damage to adjacent materials.

If the window can be retrofitted by adding or applying an energy conservation measure, the preservation requirements can be met if the following conditions apply:

- The window's condition is first evaluated to determine the physical effect retrofitting will have on the sash and frame (introducing rabbets for weatherseals and secondary glazing panels may not be acceptable in all cases).
- Measures that promote condensation, such as installing interior storms, secondary sash glazing, and thermal shutters and shades without adequate ventilation are avoided.
- The visual impact of the measure is considered within the context of the regulatory agency (exterior storm windows, for example, may not be permitted in certain cases).

If the condition of the existing window dictates replacement, be sure to do the following:

- Replicate the existing unit, in material and detail, as closely as possible.
- Evaluate the new unit's cost, durability, maintenance requirements, and appearance, in addition to anticipated energy performance.

In the case of a landmark building do not rule out a selective approach combining two or more of the options given. Wholesale window rehabilitation programs often draw attention away from the specific condition of individual windows, resulting in unnecessary destruction of original window fabric and delays or denials of approval from landmark agencies.

# Rehabilitation Standards and Guidelines

The U.S. Department of the Interior has developed 10 standards that evaluate alterations to historic properties listed in the National Register of Historic Places. In addition, the standards are used to determine eligibility of income-producing properties for federal tax benefits. The standards, which have been used widely by states and local communities as well as by the federal government, apply to both the exterior and interior of historic buildings, their design and construction, the materials used, and sites, landscapes, and archeological resources.

A set of advisory guidelines, which gives examples of rehabilitation procedures that are recommended or not recommended, helps direct the process of adhering to the 10 standards. These guidelines include specific recommendations for the repair or replacement of windows in historic buildings as well as for the addition of windows to accommodate a new use.

## Secretary of the Interior's Standards for Rehabilitation

1. A property shall be used for its historic purpose or be placed in a new use that requires minimal change to the defining characteristics of the building and its site and environment.

2. The historic character of a property shall be retained and preserved. The removal of historic materials or alteration of features and spaces that characterize a property shall be avoided.

3. Each property shall be recognized as a physical record of its time, place, and use. Changes that create a false sense of historical development, such as adding conjectural features or architectural elements from other buildings, shall not be undertaken.

4. Most properties change over time; those changes that have acquired historic significance in their own right shall be retained and preserved.

5. Distinctive features, finishes, and construction techniques or examples of craftsmanship that characterize a historic property shall be preserved.

6. Deteriorated historic features shall be repaired rather than replaced. Where the severity of deterioration requires replacement of a distinctive feature, the new feature shall match the old in design, color,

texture, and other visual qualities and, where possible, materials. Replacement of missing features shall be substantiated by documentary, physical, or pictorial evidence.

7. Chemical or physical treatments, such as sandblasting, that cause damage to historic material shall not be used. The surface cleaning of structures, if appropriate, shall be undertaken using the gentlest means possible.

8. Significant archeological resources affected by a project shall be protected and preserved. If such resources must be disturbed, mitigation measures shall be undertaken.

9. New additions, exterior alterations, or related new construction shall not destroy historic materials that characterize the property. The new work shall be differentiated from the old and shall be compatible with the massing, size, scale, and architectural features to protect the historic integrity of the property and its environment.

10. New additions and adjacent or related new construction shall be undertaken in such a manner that if removed in the future, the essential form and integrity of the historic property and its environment would be unimpaired.

## GUIDELINES FOR REHABILITATING WINDOWS IN HISTORIC BUILDINGS

A highly decorative window with an unusual shape, glazing pattern, or color is most likely identified immediately as a character-defining feature of the building. It is far more difficult, however, to assess the importance of repeated windows on a facade, particularly if they are individually simple in design and material, such as the large, multi-paned sash of many industrial buildings. Because rehabilitation projects frequently include proposals to replace window sash or even entire windows to improve thermal efficiency or to create a new appearance, it is essential that their contribution to the overall historic character of the building be assessed together with their physical condition before specific repair or replacement work is undertaken.

### Recommended

Identifying, retaining, and preserving windows—and their functional and decorative features—that are important in defining the overall historic character of the building. Such features can include frames, sash, muntins, glazing, sills, heads, hoodmolds, panelled or decorated jambs and moldings, and interior and exterior shutters and blinds.

Protecting and maintaining the wood and architectural metal which comprise the window frame, sash, muntins, and surrounds through appropriate surface treatments such as cleaning, rust removal, limited paint removal, and reapplication of protective coating systems.

Making windows weathertight by recaulking and replacing or

installing weatherstripping. These actions also improve thermal efficiency.

Evaluating the overall condition of materials to determine whether more than protection and maintenance are required, i.e., if repairs to windows and window features will be required.

Repairing window frames and sash by patching, splicing, consolidating or otherwise reinforcing. Such repair may also include replacement in kind of those parts that are either extensively deteriorated or are missing when there are surviving prototypes such as architraves, hoodmolds, sash, sills, and interior or exterior shutters and blinds.

Replacing in kind an entire window that is too deteriorated to repair—if the overall form and detailing are still evident—using the physical evidence to guide the new work. If using the same kind of material is not technically or economically feasible, then a compatible substitute material may be considered.

### Not Recommended

Removing or radically changing windows which are important in defining the overall historic character of the building so that, as a result, the character is diminished.

Changing the number, location, size or glazing pattern of windows, through cutting new openings, blocking-in windows, and installing replacement sash that does not fit the historic window opening.

Changing the historic appearance of windows through the use of inappropriate designs, materials, finishes, or colors which radically change the sash, depth of reveal, and muntin configuration; the reflectivity and color of the glazing; or the appearance of the frame.

Obscuring historic window trim with metal or other material.

Stripping windows of historic material such as wood, iron, cast iron, and bronze.

Failing to provide adequate protection of materials on a cyclical basis so that deterioration of the windows results.

Retrofitting or replacing windows rather than maintaining the sash, frame, and glazing.

Failing to undertake adequate measures to assure the preservation of historic windows.

Replacing an entire window when repair of materials and limited replacement of deteriorated or missing parts are appropriate.

Failing to reuse serviceable window hardware such as brass lifts and sash locks.

Using substitute material for the replacement part that does not convey the visual appearance of the surviving parts of the window or that is physically or chemically incompatible.

Removing a character-defining window that is unrepairable and blocking it in; or replacing it with a new window that does not convey the same visual appearance.

*Design for Missing Historic Features*

**Recommended**

Designing and installing new windows when the historic windows (frame, sash, and glazing) are completely missing. The replacement windows may be an accurate restoration using historical, pictorial, and physical documentation; or be a new design that is compatible with the window openings and the historic character of the building.

**Not Recommended**

Creating a false historical appearance because the replaced window is based on insufficient historical, pictorial, and physical documentation.

Introducing a new design that is incompatible with the historic character of the building.

*Alterations/Additions for the New Use*

**Recommended**

Designing and installing additional windows on rear or other non-character-defining elevations if required by the new use. New window openings may also be cut into exposed party walls. Such design should be compatible with the overall design of the building but should not duplicate the fenestration pattern and detailing of a character-defining elevation.

Providing a setback in the design of dropped ceilings when they are required for the new use to allow for the full height of the window openings.

**Not Recommended**

Installing new windows, including frames, sash, and muntin configuration, that are incompatible with the building's historic appearance or obscure, damage, or destroy character-defining features.

Inserting new floors or furred-down ceilings which cut across the glazed areas of windows so that the exterior form and appearance of the windows are changed.

# NOTES

Chapter 1: WINDOWS IN AMERICAN ARCHITECTURE: A HISTORICAL OVERVIEW

[1] John C. Poppeliers, S. Allen Chambers, Jr., and Nancy B. Schwartz, *What Style Is It?* (Washington, D.C.: The Preservation Press, 1983); Virginia and Lee McAllester, *A Field Guide to American Houses* (New York: Alfred A. Knopf, 1988).

[2] This chapter draws on a research report, partially previously published, prepared by Susan Swiatosz and Mark Segalla for this manual. See Susan Swiatosz, "A Technical History of Late Nineteenth-Century Windows in the United States," *Association of Preservation Technology Journal* 17,1 (1985).

[3] Quoted in John Peter, *Design with Glass* (New York: Reinhold Publishing Company, 1964), p. 7.

[4] John D. Stewart, Richard Pieper, Michael J. Devonshire, Callie Langham, David A. Rosen, and Marilyn A. Simon, "The Schermerhorn Row Block: A Study in Nineteenth-Century Building Technology in New York City," report prepared by the New York State Office of Parks, Recreation and Historic Preservation Bureau of Historic Sites, October 1981. A section of this report, "Window Construction on the Schermerhorn Row Block," was published in *The Window Workbook for Historic Buildings* (Washington, D.C.: Historic Preservation Education Foundation, 1986), pp. 2-8–2-48.

[5] R. G. Hatfield, *The American House Carpenter* (New York: Wiley and Putnam, 1844), pp. 352–53.

[6] Edward Shaw, *Civil Architecture* (Boston: Lincoln and Edmands, 1831), p. 110.

[7] Hatfield, pp. 352–53.

[8] A. J. Downing, *The Architecture of Country Houses* (1850; reprint, New York: Dover, 1969), p. 77.

[9] Ibid., p. 366.

[10] James H. Monckton, *The National Carpenter and Joiner* (New York: Excelsior Publishing House, 1873), pl. 45.

[11] Cited in Paine Lumber Company, *Catalog Combining Price List and Designs* (Oshkosh, Wis.: Paine Lumber Company, 1891), p. 11.

[12] Howard V. Bowen, "The Modern Use of Casement Windows," *The Brickbuilder*, 23,4 (April 1914).

[13] Howarth Reversible Sash and Sash Center Company, *Catalog* (Detroit: Howarth Reversible Sash and Sash Center Company, n.d.).

Chapter 2: EVALUATING WINDOW CONDITIONS AND PROBLEMS

[1] H. E. Beckett and A. Godfrey, *Windows: Performance, Design, and Installation* (New York: Van Nostrand Reinhold Company, 1974 ).

Chapter 3: MAINTAINING, REPAIRING, AND RETROFITTING WINDOWS

[1] Kay D. Weeks and David W. Look, "Exterior Paint Problems on Historic Woodwork" (Washington, D.C.: National Park Service, 1982), pp. 4-7.

[2] Sharon C. Park, "The Repair and Thermal Upgrading of Historic Steel Windows" (Washington, D.C.: National Park Service, n.d.).

[3] Fred Langa, Bob Flower, and Dave Sellers, "Caulk Talk," *Rodale's New Shelter* 4, 2 (February 1983), pp. 40–48.

[4] Stuart Fullerton and Rita Mahon, "Determining Energy Conservation of Window Management Systems," *Window Energy Systems* (March 1983); note 12. This industry publication provides some payback figures for 1983. Shades that fitted snugly and with an appropriate seal had good paybacks. The reduction of cooling load was estimated at 50 to 70 percent, while the reduction of heat loss was estimated at 30 to 45 percent. The payback for a white roller shade was 6.5 years, for a Roclon insulation blanket 2.25 years, and for a decorative quilt with insulation and seal one year. For a detailed discussion of thermal performance, see Stephen E. Selkowitz, "Thermal Performance of Insulating Window Systems," *ASHRAE Transaction*, vol. 85, part 2 (paper De-79-5, no. 5); and William A. Shurcliff, *Thermal Shutters and Shades* (Andover, Mass.: Brick House Publishing, 1980). An overview of available products is provided in Marguerite Smolen, "Treat Your Windows Right," *Rodale's New Shelter* (January 1985), pp. 96–100.

Chapter 4: REPLACING WINDOWS

[1] The various values are measured in accordance with American Society for Testing Materials (ASTM) standards: "Standard Test

Method for Rate of Air Leakage Through Exterior Windows" (ASTM E-283-83); "Standard Test Method for Structural Performance of Exterior Windows by Uniform Static Air Pressure Difference" (ASTM E-33-79); "Standard Test Method for Water Penetration of Exterior Windows by Uniform Static Air Pressure Difference" (ASTM E-33-83); "Standard Test Method for Water Penetration of Exterior Windows by Cyclic Static Air Pressure Differential" (ASTM E-547-75).

[2] The issue of stock versus custom-sized windows is addressed in Thomas Vonnier, "Next Window, Please," *Progressive Architecture* (August 1984).

[3] A good discussion of these various options appears in Russell J. Brooks, "Double Glazing in Wood Windows—The Muntin Problem," *The Window Workbook for Historic Buildings* (Washington, D.C.: Historic Preservation Education Foundation, 1986), pp. 6-1–6-6. A particular example—using insulated glass in an exact duplication—is discussed in Charles Parrott, "Replacement Wooden Sash and Frames with Insulating Glass and Integral Muntins," *Preservation Tech Notes* (Washington, D.C.: National Park Service, 1984).

[4] When the windows are made of sheet steel and the cross sections of the jamb are larger, a thermal break may be included in the installation.

Chapter 5: REHABILITATING WINDOWS IN LANDMARK BUILDINGS

[1] An excellent discussion regarding the Secretary's Standards is provided in "Standards for Rehabilitation and Guidelines for Rehabilitating Historic Building's Windows," *The Window Workbook for Historic Buildings* (Washington, D.C.: Historic Preservation Education Foundation, 1986).

[2] Charles E. Fisher, "Rehabilitating Windows in Historic Buildings: An Overview." In *The Window Handbook: Successful Strategies for Rehabilitating Windows in Historic Buildings* (Washington, D.C. and Atlanta, Ga.: National Park Service and Georgia Institute of Technology, 1986).

# GLOSSARY

**Acrylic**   Also plexiglass. A clear rigid plastic sheet material commonly used for safety glazing and inside storm panels.

**Active Solar Device**   A solar-energy collector, storage, or distribution system that uses fans, pumps, sensors, and controls to move fluids (water, air, and antifreeze solutions) in the collector system. See also passive solar device.

**Air Change Rate**   The rate of replacement of air in a space, usually due to infiltration of outdoor air through cracks around windows and doors; commonly expressed in air changes per hour.

**Air Film**   Also film coefficient. The layer of air next to a surface, such as a glass pane, that offers some resistance to heat flow. The R-value of a still-air film is about 0.68. See also R-value.

**Air Infiltration**   Outdoor air leaking into a structure uncontrollably because of cracks in the structure, mainly around door and window frames. Air infiltration will increase greatly as the air pressure increases because of increased wind velocity. In a well-built house the air infiltration may be less than one-half air change per hour (less than 50 percent of the inside air will be displaced by air from the outside). In a poorly built house, air infiltration could be as high as two or more air changes an hour.

**Aluminum-Clad Window**   A window with wood construction covered with an aluminum sheet and having a factory-applied finish, which provides a longer maintenance-free life.

**Anchor Strip**   A board around the window frame that is nailed to the house framing; it also serves as a windbreak. In newer windows the anchor strip may be plastic or metal.

**Apron**   The horizontal trim board under the window stool.

**AWI Seal**   The seal of the Architectural Woodwork Institute attached to a window or sash unit signifying that the assembler has complied with certain quality standards for that unit.

**Awning**   A canvas or metal shading device on a metal frame mounted on the outside of the window; an effective sunshade, especially for east and west windows.

**Awning Window**   A top-hinged sash introduced in the 1950s.

**Backband**   Also backbend. The millwork around the outside edge of the window casing, usually used when the casing consists of flat boards.

**Balance**   See sash balance.

**Balance Spring**   A device for counterbalancing a sliding sash, generally associated with a double-hung window, so that it can be held open at a position. See sash balance.

**Basement Window**   Also basement sash, cellar sash. A wood or metal in-swinging sash hinged at either the top or the bottom.

**Bay Window**   Windows that project out from the wall and extend to the ground. An angle bay window refers to the angle of departure from the plane of the wall. See also bow window.

**Bead**   A sealant or compound after application in a joint, irrespective of the method of application, such as caulking bead, glazing bead, and so forth. Also, a molding or stop used to hold glass or panels in position.

**Bedding**   A method of glazing in which a thin layer of putty or glazing compound is placed in the glass rabbet, the glass pressed into the bed, the glazier's points are driven, and the sash is face puttied; excess putty on the reverse side is removed.

**Bevel**   A cut made at an angle other than a right angle.

**Bill of Material**   A list of pieces required for millwork items, including number, size, species and grade of wood or type of metal sash, and necessary hardware.

**Blind**   A roller shade on the inside of the window. See also shutter.

**Block**   A small piece of wood, lead, neoprene, or other suitable material used to position the glass or other units in the frame.

**Bottom Rail**   The bottom horizontal member of a window sash.

**Bow Window**   Also compass window, radial bay window. A rounded bay window that projects from the wall in the shape of an arc; commonly consisting of five sash. See also bay window.

**Boxed Mullion**   A hollow mullion between two double-hung windows to hold the sash weights.

**Box-Head Window**   A window made so that the sash can slide vertically into the wall space above the head.

**Boxing**   An enclosure at the side of the window frame for holding a boxing shutter when folded.

**Box Window Frame**   See weight box.

**Brace**   Also angle brace. A wood member nailed across a window frame at the upper corner while the frame is in a squared position in order to maintain squareness while in transit before installation.

**Brick Molding**   A standard milled wood trim piece to cover the gap between the window frame and masonry.

**Brise-Soleil**   An architectural device such as a projection, louvers, or a screen to block unwanted sunlight from a building.

**British Thermal Unit (BTU)**   A heat unit equal to the amount of heat required to raise one pound of water 1°F. The abbreviation BTUH indicates BTUs per hour or a rate of heat flow.

**Bull's-Eye Glass**   A sheet of glass with a raised center formed by the blow pipe; because of its imperfections, it was used in barns and secondary windows. See crown glass.

**Bull's-Eye Window**   Also oculus, rose, wheel, oeil-de-boeuf. See cameo window.

**Bundling**   Tying the same or different parts of a window frame for shipping.

**Butt Joint**   A joint in which two simple edges touch each other and the sealant is placed into tension or compression.

**Butyl Rubber**   A co-polymer of isobutene and isoprene. As a sealant it has low recovery and slow cure but good tensile strength and elongation.

**Cabinet Sash**   Also cupboard sash. A sash door used in cabinets, often with glass.

**Cabinet Window**   A projecting window for the display of goods, as in a shop.

**Cameo Window**   A fixed oval window, generally with surrounding moldings and ornaments, often found on Colonial Revival houses.

**Cames**   Lead strips that hold small pieces of glass in leaded windows.

**Cap**   A decorative molded projection or cornice covering the lintel of a window.

**Casement**   A window sash that swings open on side hinges; in-swinging sash are of French origin, while out-swinging sash are of English origin.

**Casement Adjuster**   A device for holding a casement in any open position.

**Casement Stay**   Bar for holding a casement in any of several fixed open positions.

**Casement Window**   A window with one or more casements.

**Casing**   Also trim. Exposed molding or framing around a window or door, on either the inside or the outside, to cover the space between the window frame or jamb and the wall.

**Catch**   See latch.

**Caulking**   A mastic compound for filling joints and sealing cracks to prevent leakage of water and air; commonly made of acrylic or silicone-, bituminous-, or rubber-based material.

**Center-Hung Sash**   A sash that pivots on pins in the middle of the sash stiles and sides of the window frame to allow access for cleaning from the inside.

**Chain**   Also sash chain. Metal links running over a pulley and connecting the sash to a sash weight. Also, a restraining link in old casement or hopper windows. See sash balance.

**Channel**   A three-sided, U-shaped opening in a sash or frame to receive a light or panel, with or without removable stop or stops. (Contrasted to a rabbet, which is a two-sided, L-shaped section, as in a face-glazed window sash).

**Channel Depth**   The measurement from the bottom of the channel to the top of the stop or from sight line to the base of the channel.

**Channel Glazing**   The sealing of the joints around lights or panels set in a U-shaped channel using removable stops.

**Channel Width**   The measurement between stationary stops, or between a stationary stop and a removable stop, in a U-shaped channel.

**Check Rail**   See meeting rail.

**Chicago Window**   A large fixed sash flanked by a narrow, often movable sash on either side; first used by Chicago School architects in the late 19th and early 20th centuries.

**Clerestory**   Also clearstory, high-light window. A window in the upper part of a lofty room that admits light to the center of the room.

**Closure Strip**   A member to fill or close a space; an in-fill piece.

**Coated Glass**   A window glass with an outside surface provided with a mirror-reflective surface; the shading coefficient ranges from 20 to 45 percent. See also shading coefficient.

**Combination Window Unit**   Also combination storm sash and screen. A window assembly containing a half screen and two glass storm panels; in summer the bottom storm panel is stored in the top frame, exposing the screen panel.

**Commercial Standard**   A voluntary set of rules and regulations covering the quality or installation of a product, methods of testing, rating the product, certification, and labeling of manufactured products.

**Compound**   A formulation of ingredients, usually grouped as vehicle or polymer pigment and fillers, to produce caulking compound, elastomeric joint sealant, and so forth.

**Compression**   The pressure exerted on a compound in a joint, as by placing a light or panel in place against bedding or placing a stop in position against a bead of compounds.

**Condensation**   Droplets of water and sometimes frost (in extremely cold climates) that accumulate on the inside of the exterior covering of a building.

**Conduction**   A method of heat transfer in which heat moves through a solid.

**Convection**   A method of heat transfer in which heat moves by motion of a fluid or gas, usually air.

**Cope**   To cut the end of a member to fit the shape or molding of another member; for example, the ends of rails are coped to fit the stiles.

**Cord**   Also sash cord. In old double-hung windows a rope running over a pulley and connecting the sash to a sash weight to counterbalance the sash. See also sash balance.

**Coupled Window**   Also double window. Two separate windows separated by a mullion.

**Cove Molding**   Trim molding with a concave face.

**Crack Perimeter**   Also crackage. The total length of the crack around a sash through which outdoor air could leak into the room. In a double-hung window the total crackage is three times the width plus two times the height of the sash.

**Crown Glass**   Also bottle glass, bull's-eye glass. Large panes that first became available in the 17th century and were incorporated in wood sash windows. The glass was hand-blown through a pipe (pontil) into a circular disc, leaving a bubble or bullion where the pipe was inserted.

**Crystal Glass**   A clear glass containing lead and having a high index of refraction; seldom used in windows because of cost.

**Cylinder Glass**   A glass blown in the shape of a cylinder and flattened into a sheet.

**Design Heat Loss**   The calculated values, expressed in units of BTU per hour (abbreviated BTUH), for the heat transmitted from a warm interior to a cold outdoor condition under some prescribed extreme weather conditions. The values are useful for selecting heating equipment and estimating seasonal energy requirements. Infiltration heat loss is a part of the design heat loss.

**Desiccant**   A drying agent, such as silica gel, used by some manufacturers between the panes of insulated glass to prevent fogging between the panes.

**Dew Point Temperature**   The temperature of the air at which the water vapor in the air starts to condense as a liquid or as frost.

**Diffusing Glass**   Glass with an irregular surface for scattering light; used for privacy or to reduce glare.

**Double-Hung Window**   Window with two vertically moving sash, each closing a different part of the window.

**Double-Strength Glass**   Sheet glass with a thickness of between 0.115 to 0.133 inches (3 to 3.38 millimeters).

**Double Windows**   Also double glazing. Two windows, such as a regular window plus a storm sash, or an insulating window with air space between panes.

**Double Window**   Also coupled window. Two windows separated by a mullion, forming a unit.

**Drip Cap**   A horizontal molding to divert water from the top casing so that it drips beyond the outside of the frame.

**Drop Window**   A vertical window in which the sash can descend into a cavity in the wall below the sill.

**Dry-Bulb Temperature**   The temperature of the air as determined by a dry thermometer bulb. See sling psychrometer.

**Dry Glazing**   A form of glazing in which the glass is secured in the frame with a dry gasket, wood stops, or metal stops instead of with a glazing compound. See also reglet.

**Dust Pad**   Weatherstrip applied to the bottom of the meeting rail to reduce infiltration.

**Energy Efficiency**   The amount of output of activity per unit of energy consumed. When applied to air conditioners, it is the cooling output (BTU) divided by kilowatt input.

173

**Extension Blind Stop**   Also blind stop extender, blind casing. A molded window frame member, usually of the same thickness as the blind stop and united with it, thus increasing the width of the blind stop in order to close the gap between the window frame and the rough opening in the house frame; used to attach the window frame to the wood framing. See also reversible extension blind stop.

**Extension Casement Hinge**   A hinge for a casement window that provides clearance for cleaning the two sides of the sash from the inside.

**Extension Jamb**   Also jamb lining, jamb extender. A board used to increase the depth of the jambs of a window frame to fit a wall of any given thickness.

**Exterior Glazing**   Glass installed from the exterior of the building.

**Exterior Stop**   The removable molding or bead that holds the light or panel in place when it is on the exterior side of the light or panel.

**Face Glazing**   Glazing set with putty in an L-shaped or rabbetted frame.

**Fanlight**   A semicircular window over a door or window, with bars that spread out from the center like an open fan.

**False Window**   Also blank window, blind window. An imitation window thatserves no purpose other than to give the appearance of a window for symmetry or for decoration.

Fasteners   Devices for joining two parts together, such as screws, nails, and bolts.

**Fenestration**   The placement of window openings in a building wall; one of the important elements in controlling a building's exterior appearance.

**Fillet**   A small narrow band of wood between two flutes or parallel grooves in a wood member; also the flat surface of a trim piece.

**Fin**   An outward-projecting leg located between the perimeter edges of a frame.

**Finger Joint**   A wood end joint formed by a set of interlocking fingers, coated with adhesive and meshed together under pressure.

**Finish Casing**   Also finish trim. Interior trim boards around a window unit.

**Fire Window**   A window with a fire-endurance rating specified for the location.

**Fixed Light**   Also fixed sash. A window that does not open.

**Flange**   The finlike projection around the exterior perimeter edge of a frame.

**Flashing**   Sheet metal provided for water drainage and to prevent water penetration into a building.

**Flat Glass**   Also window glass, plate glass, float glass, rolled glass, cylinder glass. Glass sold in flat sheets and named according to the method used in its manufacture.

**Float Glass**   Smooth glass formed on top of molten tin surface; a flat glass sheet.

**Flush Glazing**   Glazing that is flush with a frame.

**Fluted Rolled Glass**   A sheet of glass impressed with narrow flute patterns.

**Folding Casement**   Casement windows hinged together so they can fold into a confined space.

**Folding Shutter**   Also boxing shutter. A folding shutter that, when folded, fits into an enclosure at the side of the window.

**Forced Convection**   A heat transfer process aided by mechanical circulation of a liquid (such as water) or of a gas (such as air). This term applies to natural wind flow over a window.

**Framing**   Structural members to provide a window opening.

**French Window**   Two casement sash hinged on the sides to open in the middle; the sash extends to the floor and serves as a door to a porch or terrace.

**Friction Hinge**   A window hinge that remains open at any position by means of friction in the hinge.

**Gable Sash**   A fixed sash in the gable of a building that admits light into an attic.

**Gasket**   A preformed shape of rubber or rubberlike composition used to fill and seal a joint opening either alone or with supplemental application of a sealant.

**Glass**   An elastic transparent material composed of silica (sand), soda (sodium carbonate), and lime (calcium carbonate) with small quantities of aluminina, boric, or magnesia oxides.

**Glass Brick**   Glass that has been pressed into a hollow brick form, usually installed in a wall opening or as a decorative structure.

**Glazier's Point**   Also sprig. A thin metal triangle with one point pounded into the frame to hold the glass; putty is then applied to seal the glass.

**Glazing**   The securing of glass in prepared openings in windows, door panels, screens, partitions, and so forth.

**Glazing Bead**   Also glass stop, wood stop, sill bead. A removable trim that holds the glass in place.

**Glazing Channel**   A groove cut into the sash for the mounting of glass.

**Glazing Clip**   A metal clip for holding glass in a metal frame while putty is applied.

**Glazing Compound**   A material used to seal panes of glass in the frame; a modern substitute for putty.

**Glazing Gasket**   A special extruded plastic shape for attaching window glass to metal or masonry wall openings. It serves also as a cushion and insulator.

**Groove**   A long, narrow cut on the face of a wood member; a groove across the grain is a dado, while one parallel with the grain is a plough. A groove exposes three surfaces, in contrast with the two surfaces exposed in a rabbet or notching. See also rabbetted joint, plough.

**Ground**   A wood strip around a window frame used to measure the thickness of plaster during plastering.

**Ground Casing**   A molding around the window frame that attaches the frame to studs and header and furnishes a ground for plastering; used especially in old windows.

**Ground Glass**   A light-diffusing glass, usually sandblasted or ground.

**Ground Light**   The reflection of skylight or sunlight from the ground.

**Head**   The top member of a window or door frame.

**Head Casing**   The horizontal exposed framing across the top of the window. See also Casing.

**Header**   Also lintel, beam. Supporting member or beam above a window opening that transfers building weight above to the supporting wall structure on each side of the window. "Header" generally refers to a wood beam, whereas "lintel" often refers to a steel beam.

**Head Flashing**   Flashing installed in a wall over a window.

**Head Jamb**   Also head. All the horizontal members at the top of the window frame.

**Heat-Absorbing Glass**   Also tinted glass. Gray, bronze, or blue-green tinted window glass containing chemicals that absorb light and heat radiation and reduce glare and brightness. Shading coefficient of this glass varies from about 50 to 70 percent.

**Heat Mirror**   A thin transparent insulating film inserted between double glazing that permits transmission of visible light but reflects far-infrared radiation.

**Heat Transfer**   The exchange of heat through building materials.

**Heat-Transfer Conduction**   Heat transfer through a solid. A typical example is when a metal spoon is placed in a hot cup of liquid; the portion of the metal spoon not submerged heats up quickly by conduction. In houses heat loss by conduction occurs typically through window panes. To slow this heat transfer, double-pane glass is used.

**Heat-Transfer Convection**   Heat transfer from one object to another by the movement of air, water, or another fluid.

**Heat-Transfer Radiation**   Heat transfer across space by radiation whenever one object is warmer than another.

**Heat-Transfer Coefficient**   Also U-value. A value indicating the rate of heat flow through a building, expressed in units of BTUH per square foot of surface per 1°F difference between indoor and outdoor air temperature. This is numerically equal to the inverse of the sum of R-values for the building.

**Hood**   A decorative cover placed over a window to protect it. See also cap.

**Hopper Light**   Also hopper vent, hopper ventilator. Inward-opening sash hinged at the bottom.

**Horn**  See stile lug.

**Hung Window**  Window with one or more hanging sashes.

**Hygroscopic**  The ability to give off and take on moisture, as in wood exposed to changes in the relative humidity of the air.

**Infiltration Heat Loss**  The loss, expressed in units of BTUH, resulting from leakage of outdoor air into a structure and the escape of indoor air. The loss depends on the indoor and outdoor temperatures, the crack perimeter, and the rate of air leakage per foot of crack. See also design heat loss.

**Infrared Heat Detector**  An optical device that can show areas of large heat leakages from buildings, such as windows, doors, and poorly insulated walls.

**Inset Dormer**  See dormer window.

**Insulating Glass**  Double or triple glazing with an enclosed, dehydrated, and hermetically sealed air space between the panes; the space is commonly between ³⁄₁₆ and ¾ inch.

**Insulating Pane**  An interior or exterior covering, door, shutter, or sash to increase the thermal resistance of a window; commonly a nontransparent panel inserted seasonally or during night hours only.

**Insulating Strip**  A strip of insulating material separating metal storm sash from metal window sash. Also, a plastic separator between two panes of insulating glass.

**Interior Glazing**  Glass installed on the interior of a building.

**Interior Stop**  The removable molding or bead that holds the light in place when it is on the interior side of the light.

**Interior Venetian Blind**  A venetian blind installed between two panes of glass and remotely controlled.

**Jamb**  The vertical member of a frame adjacent to the structural members of a building.

**Jamb Anchor**  A device to anchor or set the window frame to the wall.

**Jamb Depth**  The width of the window frame from inside to outside.

**Jamb Horn**  The part of the jamb of the window frame extending beyond the sill or head jamb.

**Label**  A projecting molding by the sides and over the top of an opening. See also hood mold.

**Label Stop**  An ornamental projection on each end of a label, sill, or sill course. It often takes the shape of a gargoyle or other decorative carving.

**Labeled Window**  Window bearing fire-rating label of Underwriters' Laboratories.

**Laminated Glass**  See shatterproof glass.

**Latch**  Also catch, look. A device that holds a window shut, such as the latch at the meeting rail of a double-hung window or one mounted on the stile of casement windows.

**Lattice**  Wood or plastic strips set diagonally in a window pane to give the effect of a lattice window.

**Lattice Window**    Also lozenge. A window with glazing bars set diagonally.

**Law of Reflection**    A scientific axiom stating that the angle of incidence of light is equal to the angle of reflection when radiation hits a reflecting surface.

**Laylight**    A glazed ceiling opening for lighting.

**Lead Light**    Also lead glazing, stained glass. A window with small panes of glass set in grooved rods of cast lead or cames. The glass can be clear or stained.

**Life-Cycle Cost**    The cost of equipment over its entire life, including operating and maintenance costs.

**Lift**    Also sash lift. A handle for raising the lower sash in a double-hung window.

**Light**    Another term for a pane of glass used in a window.

**Light-Fast**    A material or surface that is color stable when exposed to sunlight.

**Lintel**    Horizontal member of wood, steel, or stone over a window opening to support the weight of the wall above. See also header.

**Lock Rail**    See meeting rail.

**Lock Stile**    The vertical member of a casement sash that closes against the surrounding frame.

**Louver**    Slanted fins or slats in a window, ventilator, or venetian blind; the slats may be fixed or adjustable and made of wood, metal, glass, or plastic.

**Lozenge**    A diamond-shaped design, as in a window composed of diamond-shaped panes. See also quarry glass.

**Lug**    See stile lug.

**Lug Sill**    A window sill extending beyond the window frame.

**Matte-Surface Glass**    Etched, ground, or sandblasted glass that provides diffused light.

**Meeting Rail**    Also check rail, lock rail. One of the two horizontal members of a double-hung sash that come together.

**Meeting Stile**    The vertical member in a pair of stiles, as in abutting casement windows.

**Member**    Any structural part of a window, such as a rail, stile, or lintel.

**Millwork**    Window sash and other wood products made in a woodworking plant.

**Miter Joint**    Two members joined at an angle, commonly 45°.

**Module**    A dimension that is repeated in construction, such as a 4-inch module for window sizes.

**Moisture Barrier**    Also vapor barrier. A material that retards the passage of water vapor from one space to another. Polyethylene sheet is commonly used as a vapor retarder.

**Moisture Content**    The percentage of the dry weight of a material composed of water, such as in wood.

**Molding**   Also mold. A relatively narrow strip of wood used to conceal a joint or emphasize the ornamentation of a structure.

**Mold Stone**   Also jamb stone. A stone serving as a window jamb.

**Morse Collector**   The earliest solar hot-air collector; patented in 1881, a window with glass in front of heavy metal plate and air openings for convected flow.

**Mortise and Tenon Joint**   Also mortise joint. Joint with an opening (mortise) into which a projection (tenon) is fitted.

**Mullion**   A horizontal or vertical member that holds together two adjacent lights of glass, units of sash, or sections of curtain wall.

**Mullion Cover**   Also mullion trim. A molding covering the vertical joint between two window frames.

**Muntin**   Also sash bar, window bar, glazing bar. A secondary framing member (horizontal, vertical, or slanted) to hold the window panes in the sash. This term is often confused with "mullion."

**Muntin Grilles**   Wood, plastic, or metal grilles designed for a single-light sash to give the appearance of muntins in a multilight sash but are removable for ease in cleaning the window.

**Multilight Sash**   A sash divided into many lights.

**Nail**   Common nails and box nails are used in window frame assembly and installation; casing nails are used for assembling heavier exterior moldings; finish nails and brads are used for interior trim members.

**Neoprene**   A polymer developed by the DuPont Company of chloroprene prepared from coat, salt, and limestone. It has excellent resistance to oxidation, ozone, sunlight, aging, heat, and cold.

**Obscure Glass**   Also visionproof glass. Any textured glass (frosted, etched, fluted, or ground) used for privacy, light diffusion, or decorative effects.

**Ogee Curve**   Also ogee molding. A reverse flex curve commonly found in window moldings or trim.

**Operator**   A crank-operated device for opening and closing casement or jalousie windows.

**Overhead Balance**   See sash balance.

**Palladian Window**   A tripartite window characterized by a large arched middle window flanked by rectangular windows.

**Pane**   A sheet of glass for glazing a window. After installation, the pane is referred to as a light or window light.

**Panel Window**   A form of picture window consisting of several sash or fixed glazings separated by crossbars, mullions, or both.

**Panning**   An applied material, usually metal, that covers the front exterior surface of an existing window frame or mullion.

**Parting Bead**   Also parting strip, parting stop. A vertical strip on each jamb that separates the sash of a double-hung window.

**Parting Slip**   A thin wood strip separating the sash weights in the weight box of each jamb of an old double-hung window.

**Passive Solar Device**   Any solar collector, storage, or distribution system that functions without a motor-driven fan or pump and without electrical sensors or controls. The basic and intrinsic solar device is a south-facing window, usually with multiple glazing, which transmits solar energy and is also required for view and ventilation. Various adaptations between   passive and active solar devices (hybrids) are evolving.

**Patterned Glass**   One or both surfaces of glass with a rolled design; used for privacy and light diffusion.

**Payback**   The time required for the cost of energy saved to equal the total cost of modification.

**Perimeter**   The outer boundary of a building or a building segment, such as a panel, glass light, or wall section.

**Perimeter Seal**   A sealer for any joint in the outer boundary of a building or building segment.

**Permeability**   The ability of a porous material to permit transmission of water vapor.

**Permeance**   A measure of the transmission of water vapor through a material; expressed in units of perms.

**Pile**   A generic term used to describe strips of woven material of various densities and heights used to function as barriers against air and water infiltration in a window or a door.

**Pivot**   The axis or hardware about which a window rotates.

**Plastics**   Artificial substances made of organic polymers that can be extruded or molded into various shapes, some of which have been adapted to windows. The material is commonly stiffer than rubber.

**Plate Glass**   High-quality ground and polished sheet glass with thicknesses from ⅛ to 1¼ inches (3.2 to 31.8 millimeters).

**Plexiglas**   Also acrylic. A trade name for a clear durable sheet plastic made of acrylic; used for safety glazing and for inside storm panels.

**Plough**   Also plow. A three-sided rectangular groove or slot cut parallel to the grain.

**Plowed-and-Bored Frame**   A box window frame in old windows where the edges of the stiles were plowed and bored to receive the sash-weight cord and tie the knot.

**Polybutene**   A light-colored liquid, straight-chain aliphatic hydro-carbon polymer that is nondrying and widely used as a major component in sealing and caulking compounds. It is essentially nonreactive and inert.

**Polyethylene**   A semitransparent plastic sheet commonly used as a vapor retarder but also as a temporary, low-cost double glazing or storm panel.

**Polyvinylchloride**   Also PVC. An extruded or molded plastic material used for window framing and as a thermal barrier for aluminum windows.

**Preservative**   A solution for protecting wood parts from the weather and consisting of wood preservative and a water repellent.

**Pressed Glass**   Glass that has been pressed into shape, such as for glass bricks. See also glass brick.

**Prime Sash**   The balanced or moving sash of a window unit.

**Prime Window**   A window with single or multiple glazing to which storm sash may be installed.

**Primer**   A special coating designed to enhance the adhesion of sealant or sealant systems to certain surfaces.

**Priming**   Sealing a porous surface so that a compound will not stain, lose elasticity, or shrink excessively because of excessive absorption into the surround. A sealant primer or surface conditioner may be used to promote adhesion of a curing sealant to certain surfaces.

**Protected Window**   An awning window that swings either inward or outward at the top or bottom. A PIB ("protect in at bottom") window can be cleaned from the inside.

**Protected Opening**   A window with a fire-resistance rating suitable for the wall in which it is located.

**Psychrometer**   See sling psychrometer.

**Psychrometric Chart**   A chart showing dry-bulb and wet-bulb temperatures used to determine the relative humidity of air and the dew point temperature. Other engineering data referring to moisture in the air are also shown.

**Pull**   A handle for opening a window.

**Pulley (Sash Pulley)**   Typically used in older windows, a sash cord attached to a sash weight was carried over this devise to a window sash. Four pulleys, located at the top of the jambs, were used for a double-hung window.

**Pulley Stile**   Part of the window frame in older windows; a removable vertical board flush with the frame to allow access to the sash weights and cord.

**Pullman Balance**   See sash balance.

**Putty**   A thick paste made of whiting and linseed oil used for sealing panes of glass in the frame. See also glazing compound.

**Quarrel**   A diamond-shaped or square glass piece set diagonally; a medieval term for small panes of glass set diagonally in Gothic windows. See also lattice window.

**Quarry Glass**   A square glass piece set diagonally.

**Quarter**   A square panel.

**Rabbet**   Also glazing rabbet. A two-sided, L-shaped recess in sash or frame to receive lights or panels. When no stop or molding is added, such rabbets are face glazed. Adding a removable stop produces a three-sided U-shaped channel.

**Rabbetted Joint**   The joint formed by two boards with rabbetted ends, as in some window frames.

**Rabbet Size**   The size of a glass opening, including clearance.

**Racking**   The movement or distortion of sash or frames caused by lack of rigidity or adjustment of ventilator sections. It puts excessive strain on the sealant and may result in joint failure.

**Radiation**   The transmission of energy through space without heating the air between, as in solar radiation.

**Radiation Cooling**   The radiant heat loss due to a temperature differential between objects—for instance, the heat loss (cooling) of a roof during the night.

**Rail**   Also head rail, top rail, bottom rail, meeting rail. A horizontal member of a window sash.

**Reflective Glass**   A window glass coated to reflect radiation striking the surface of the glass.

**Refraction**   The deflection of a light ray from a straight path when it passes at an oblique angle from one medium (such as air) to another (such as glass).

**Reglet**   Any slot cut into masonry or formed into poured concrete or precast stone. Also, an open mortar joint left between two courses of bricks or stones or a slot cut or cast into other types of building materials.

**Relative Humidity**   The weight of water vapor in air divided by the weight of water vapor in completely saturated air at the same temperature, expressed as a percentage.

**Resonance**   The sympathetic vibration, resounding, or ringing of enclosures, room surfaces, panels, and so forth when excited at their natural frequencies.

**Retrofit**   The application of sealing systems and other components for upgrading structurally sound but worn or inefficient windows to modern performance standards.

**Reveal**   The surface of a window jamb, perpendicular to the wall, or the part of the jamb from the wall to the face of the window sash.

**Reversible Extension Blind Stop**   An extension blind stop rabbeted to receive either ½- or $^{25}/_{32}$-inch sheathing.

**Reversible Window**   A window sash that can be pivoted around a vertical axis for ease of cleaning.

**Ribbon Window**   A series of windows in a row across the face of a building.

**Rolled Glass**   A flat glass having varying transparency and a patterned or irregular surface produced by rolling. Subtypes include flat wire glass, corrugated glass, and figured glass; thickness ranges from ⅛ to 1¼ inches (3.2 to 31.8 millimeters).

**Roll-Up Screen**   A screen installed on the inside of the house and operated like a roll-up shade. The screen fits into metal track on the side and rolls up into a box at the top. Another model, the roll-down screen, rolls into a box at the bottom.

**Roll-Up Shade**   Also roller shade, window blind. A window shade that rolls up around a cylindrical holder at the top and is installed on the inside of a house. Serves to maintain privacy, reflect some solar radiation, and reduce convection flow when fully extended.

**Roman Shade**   A hanging fabric over a window that serves as an insulated window shade and can be rolled enfolded or drawn upward out of the way.

**Round-Head Window**   A window with a rounded top member.

**Roundel**   A very small circular window; also a circular light resembling the bottom of a bottle. See bull's-eye window.

**Rowlock**   Also roloc. A sill made from brick and installed on a slant in the direction of the rainfall.

**R-Value**   Also thermal resistance. A measure of resistance to heat flow of a material or building; a higher value indicates a better heat-insulating property. The R-value of an ordinary single-pane sash with 15 miles-per-hour wind on one side is about O.9.

**Saddle Bar**   A light steel bar placed horizontally across a window to stiffen leaded glazing.

**Saddle Bead**   A glazing bead for securing two panes.

**Safety Glass**   A strengthened or reinforced glass that is less susceptible to breaking or splintering, such as glass for storm doors and some windows. See also tempered glass, shatterproof glass, and plexiglass.

**Safety Lintel**   A second lintel of wood behind a stone lintel in a window opening.

**Sash**   The frame, including rabbets and muntin bars, if used, to receive lights of glass either with or without removable stops and designed either for face or channel glazing.

**Sash Adjuster**   See casement adjuster.

**Sash Balance**   A device for counterbalancing a sash of a double-hung window to hold it open. There are four basic types: (1) spiral—a balance using a spirally wound spring; (2) spring—a balance introduced in the 1890s using a spring for counterbalancing; (3) coiled tape (also pullman balance, overhead balance)—a coiled steel tape under spring tension for balancing the sash, located in the head jamb of the window frame; and (4) counterweight—the most common type of balancing system, using a weight held by a sash rope or chain over a pulley.

**Sash Center**   A supporting device of two parts for horizontally pivoted sash.

**Sash Stop**   A molding that covers the joint between window sash and the jamb.

**Sash Weight**   A cast-iron or lead counterweight for a movable sash. See also sash balance.

**Screen Molding**   The trim for covering the edge of screening material on the frame.

**Screen-Wire Cloth**   A close-mesh woven screening material of metal, plastic, or fiberglass for a window screen that blocks the entry of insects but permits light, air, and vision through the screen.

**Screw-On Bead, Screw-On Stop**   A stop, molding, or bead that is fastened by screws rather than snapped into position without additional fastening

183

**Sealant**   A compound such as butyl tape used to fill and seal a joint or opening, as contrasted with a liquid sealer, used to seal a porous surface.

**Sealed Glass**   Two panes separated by a sealed space. See also insulating glass, thermopane.

**Setting Blocks**   Small blocks of composition, lead, or neoprene placed under the bottom edge of a light or panel to prevent its settling onto the bottom rabbet or channel after setting, thus distorting the sealant.

**Shade Screen**   Also sun screen, sun blind. A specially fabricated window screen of sheet material with small narrow louvers formed in place to intercept solar radiation striking a window; the louvers are so small that only extremely small insects can pass through. Also, an awning with fixed louvers of metal or wood construction.

**Shading Coefficient**   The decimal value of a window's solar gain divided by the solar gain for a clear single-glass window of the same size. The shading coefficient of clear double glazing is about 0.85 to 0.9.

**Shatterproof Glass**   Also laminated glass. Two sheets of glass with a transparent  plastic sheet sandwiched between them to form a pane resistant to shattering.

**Sheet Glass**   See window glass.

**Shim**   A small wedgelike device, typically a piece of an exterior wood shingle, which tightens the fit between two separate building elements.

**Show Window**   A window for display of goods. See also cabinet window.

**Shutter**   A frame assembly mounted on a window supporting a panel that shuts out light or view from a window opening; originally for protection, then decoration, and now energy conservation. Some authorities categorize solid panels as shutters and louvered panels as blinds.

**Shutter Bar**   A device for securing the shutter in place; sometimes called a shutter dog.

**Shutter Blind**   An adjustable louver on the outside of the window.

**Shutter Box**   A recessed opening on the inside of window jambs to enclose inside shutters while open.

**Side-Hung Window**   See casement window.

**Side Light**   Also margin light. A fixed, often narrow glass window next to a door opening or window.

**Side Stop**   The vertical window stop on either side of the window or door frame opening.

**Signal Sash Fastener**   A device for fastening double-hung windows that requires a long pole to reach the fastener.

**Silicone Sealant**   A sealant having as its chemical composition a backbone consisting of alternating silicon-oxygen atoms.

**Sill** Also sill plate, inside sill, outside sill. The horizontal member at the bottom of the window frame; a masonry sill or subsill can be below the sill of the window unit.

**Sill Block** A concrete or stone unit for the sill.

**Sill Course** A continuation of the masonry sills of the windows along the wall.

**Sill Drip Molding** A sill member on a window frame serving as a screen stop. Also, the extension of the sill that contains the drip cut.

**Sill Windbreak** A window frame member occasionally used to prevent air infiltration around the sill and secure the frame to the structure; generally installed in a groove in the bottom of the window frame sill immediately behind the sill siding groove.

**Simplex Casement** A casement window without hardware for opening and closing the sash.

**Single-Hung Window** A window similar to a double-hung window except that the top sash is stationary.

**Single-Strength Glass** Glass whose thickness ranges between 0.085 and 0.100 inch (2.16 and 2.57 millimeters).

**Skylight** Light received from the sky away from the sun (also sky shine). A window in the roof. A relatively new product, operable or pivoting, that allows light, ventilation, and a means of egress from attic spaces.

**Sling Psychrometer** A measuring instrument with two thermometers (dry bulb and wet bulb) used for determining the dew point and relative humidity of air; it ascertains the point at which moisture will condense on the inside surface of the glass. See also psychrometric chart.

**Slip-Head Sash Unit** A sash that slips into a hidden pocket in the wall above the frame. See box-head window.

**Slot Ventilator** An opening in the lower part of a wood storm sash for venting the air space between the main and storm sashes.

**Soft Glass** Window glass.

**Soft Light** A light that produces poorly defined shadows.

**Solar Altitude** The angle between the sun and the horizontal plane of the earth.

**Solar Heat Gain** Heat from solar radiation that enters a building.

**Solar Orientation** A building placed on a lot so that the long dimension and a majority of the windows face south.

**Solar Radiation** The total radiation of energy from the sun, including ultraviolet and infrared wavelengths as well as visible light.

**Solar Screen** A sun-shading device, such as screened panels, louvers, or blinds, installed to intercept solar radiation.

**Solid Frame** A window frame made from a single piece of lumber; rarely do old buildings use this type of frame.

**Sound Insulation** Also sound isolation. The use of building materials or construction techniques that will reduce or resist the transmission of sound.

**Sound Leak**   A hole, crack, or opening that permits the passage of sound.

**Sound-Insulating Glass**   Also sound-resistive glass. Double glass fixed on resilient mountings and separated so as to reduce sound transmission.

**Spandrel**   An exterior wall panel filling the space beneath a window sill, usually extending to the top of the window in multistory construction.

**Specification**   A written document often accompanying architectural drawings  giving such details as the scope of work, materials to be used, installation method, and quality of workmanship for work under a contract.

**Specific Heat**   The amount of heat required to raise the temperature of one pound of a given substance 1°F divided by the heat required to raise one pound of water 1°F. Also, a ration used to determine the heat-storage capacity of a substance.

**Specular Surface**   A mirrored surface that reflects light at the same angle as the light falling on the surface. See also law of reflection.

**Spiral Balance**   See sash balance.

**Splayed Window**   A window unit set at an angle to the wall.

**Spline**   A rectangular strip of wood or metal inserted between two boards that have been slotted to receive it.

**Spring**   See glazier's point.

**Spring Balance**   See sash balance.

**Spring Bolt**   A fastener for holding the sash in a fixed location by means of a spring-loaded bolt in the stile entering a hole in the jamb.

**Stacked Window Unit**   A combined grouping of awning, hopper, casement, or nonoperative windows to form a large glazed unit.

**Stationary Stop**   The permanent stop or lip of a rabbet on the side opposite to the side on which lights or panels are set.

**Stiffener**   A secondary member attached to a window to prevent a plate or frame from buckling.

**Stile**   The vertical-edge members of a window sash.

**Stile Lug**   Also lug, horn. One of two extensions of the sash stiles to support the upper sash of a double-hung window.

**Stock**   Lumber, window units, trim, and other materials in standard sizes and dimensions commonly available from suppliers.

**Stock Millwork**   Also stock size. Manufactured millwork, such as window units, sold in standard sizes and styles and available from suppliers.

**Stool**   A shelflike board of the interior part of the window sill against which the bottom rail of the sash closes.

**Stop**   Either the stationary lip at the back of a rabbet or the removable molding at the front of the rabbet, either or both serving with the help of spacers to hold a light or panel in the sash or frame.

**Stop Extender**   See extension blind stop.

**Stop Screw**  A screw for fastening a stop to the window frame.

**Storm Clip**  A device attached to the muntin of a metal sash to prevent the pane from moving outward.

**Stormproof Window**  A window for resisting high wind and precipitation.

**Storm Sash**  Also storm window. An extra window on the outside to protect an existing window but mainly to increase the window's thermal resistance.

**Storm Panel**  An exterior covering, door, shutter, or sash to protect the window during a storm.

**Structural Gasket**  A synthetic rubber section designed to engage the edge of glass or other sheet material in a surrounding frame by forcing an interlocking filler strip into a grooved recess in the face of the gasket.

**Sunburst Light**  See fanlight.

**Sun-Control Film**  A tinted or reflective film applied to the inside surface of window glass, reducing visible and ultraviolet light and blocking solar radiation. Shading coefficients can be as low as 0.25. Such films serve to reduce glare. Some can be removed and reapplied with changing seasons.

**Sweep Lock**  A sash fastener, located at the meeting rails of a double-hung window, which rotates and clamps the two rails closer together.

**Tape Balance**  See sash balance.

**Tempered Glass**  Special heat-treated, high-strength safety glass that shatters into pebble-sized particles but not into slivers.

**Tension Jamb**  A device, introduced in the 1930s, that applies constant tension to the sash to hold it in place; used instead of sash weights.

**Tension Screen**  A screen installed on the window without a side frame or side tracks. It is fastened at the top with hooks; a tensioning device, easily released, holds the screen at the bottom.

**Therm**  In technical usage a convenient measure of heating value, namely 100,000 BTU. One therm is roughly equivalent to the heating value of 100 cubic feet of natural (methane) gas.

**Thermal Break**  Also thermal barrier. A material of high thermal resistance placed between two metal sash or installed between adjoining metal framing of metal windows to reduce thermal conduction from indoors to outdoors.

**Thermal Conduction**  Heat transfer through a material by the contact of molecules; heat flows from a high-temperature area to one of lower temperature.

**Thermal Conductivity**  Heat-transfer property of materials expressed in units of BTUH per inch of thickness per square foot of surface per 1°F temperature difference; referred to by the letter k.

**Thermal Conductance**  Same as thermal conductivity except thickness is as stated rather than per inch; referred to by the letter C.

**Thermal Expansion**   A change in the dimension of a material as a result of temperature change.

**Thermal Insulation**   A material that resists heat flow and thus has a high R-value.

**Thermal Radiation**   Heat transfer through space without contact with a solid substance, as in solar radiation through empty space.

**Thermopane**   A trade name of an insulating glass or double glazing.

**Top Hung-In Window**   An awning window having a pivoted top sash and an in-swinging bottom sash.

**Transom**   Also transom bar. A horizontal member separating a door from a window panel above the door or separating one window above another.

**Trellis Window**   See lattice window.

**Trim**   The visible molding surrounding a window opening. See also casing.

**Triple Glazing**   Three panes of glass having air spaces between them and commonly  consisting of an insulating glass with a separate storm sash. Also available as an insulating window in a single frame.

**Triple Window**   A term generally referring to any tripartite group of windows with square heads. Frequently found on Colonial Revival houses, triple windows suggest Palladian windows but are less expensive to build.

**T-Slot**   The integral web of a window frame or sash member used to retain weatherstripping.

**Twindow**   A trade name for an insulating glass or double glazing.

**U-Value**   The amount of heat in the summer conducted from the inside air through the window configuration to the outside air or vice versa. A 15 mile-per-hour outside wind is assumed in the winter; a 7½ mile-per-hour outside wind is assumed in the summer. The air inside is assumed to be still both summer and winter. The value is expressed in BTUs per square foot based on the difference in readings between the outside and inside temperatures. For example, a U-value of 0.50 means 0.50 BTUs pass through each square foot of window configuration every hour and for each difference of 1°F between the inside and outside temperature.

**Vapor Barrier**   A membrane or coating that resists passage of water vapor from a region of high vapor pressure to low pressure; more accurately called a vapor retarder.

**Vapor Pressure**   The part of the total pressure of air that is due to the presence of water vapor. Vapor travels from a region of high vapor pressure to low vapor pressure.

**Venetian Blind**   A light-controlling shading device consisting of overlapping thin horizontal slats that can be raised or adjusted from wide open to closed positions by varying the tilt of the slats. See also interior venetian blind.

188

**Venetian Window**   See Palladian window.

**Vent Light**   Also vent sash, night vent. A small pane in a larger sash that can be opened to provide ventilation even with the larger sash closed.

**View Sash**   A picture window with the lights divided by muntins.

**Vinyl**   See polyvinylchloride.

**Visible Spectrum**   The portion of total radiation that is visible to the human eye and that lies between the ultraviolet and the infrared portions of the electromagnetic spectrum. The colors associated with the visible spectrum include violet, indigo, blue, green, yellow, orange, and red.

**Vision-Proof Glass**   See obscure glass.

**Vista Window**   See stationary sash.

**Wash Cut**   A beveled cut in a stone sill to divert water.

**Water Drip**   A molding sometimes used on the exterior surface of an inswinging casement sash to prevent water from being driven in over the sill.

**Weatherseal**   A device that reduces the leakage of outdoor air and precipitation around the window frame into the structure.

**Weatherstrip**   A strip of resilient material for covering the joint between the window sash and frame in order to reduce air leaks and prevent water from entering the structure.

**Weep Cut**   Also drip cut. A groove in the underside of a horizontal board or masonry unit, such as a sill, which projects beyond the wall surface below to prevent water from moving back toward the wall surface.

**Weep Hole**   An opening at the base of a cavity wall to collect moisture and disperse it. Also, a breather put in a sealant to relieve moisture.

**Weight Box**   Also box window frame. A hollow cavity on each side of a double-hung window to hold the sash weights.

**Wet-Bulb Thermometer**   The air temperature recorded by a thermometer whose bulb is covered with a wet wick and exposed to a moving air stream. The wet-bulb temperature, when used in conjunction with the dry-bulb temperature, enables the observer to determine the relative humidity of the air. See also sling psychrometer.

**White-Lead Putty**   A high-quality putty with at least 10 percent white lead mixed with linseed oil and calcium carbonate.

**Windbreak**   An anchor strip or blind stop that reduces air leaks.

**Window Bar**   See muntin.

**Window Glass**   Also sheet glass. A glass made from soda, lime, and silica; its thickness ranges from 0.05 to 0.22 inch (1.27 to 5.9 millimeters). Three grades—AA, A, and B—are offered by glass manufacturers.

**Window Schedule**   A listing of windows required in a given house, stating types, sizes, number of lights, manufacturer, and any special needs.

**Window Unit**   A complete window with sash and frame.

**Wind Pressure**   The pressure produced by stopping the wind velocity; the main cause of air infiltration.

**Wire Glass**   A glass with inner wire mesh for strength and fire-retardant qualities.

**Wood Moisture Content**   The weight of moisture in wood compared with the weight of completely dried wood and expressed by a percentage. Moisture contents of 6 to 12 percent at the time of construction are specified in the commercial standards.

**Worm-Type Hardware**   A device for opening and closing a casement or awning-type sash by means of a crank.

**Yoke**   The head window jamb in a box window frame.

# INFORMATION SOURCES

American Society for Testing and Materials (ASTM)
1916 Race Street
Philadelphia, PA 19103
(215) 299-5496

American Society of Heating, Refrigerating and
Air-Conditioning Engineers (ASHRAE)
1791 Tullie Circle, N.E.
Atlanta, GA 30329
(404) 636-8400

Architectural Woodwork Institute
2310 South Walter Reed Drive
Arlington, VA 22206
(703) 671-9100

Flat Glass Marketing Association (FGMA)
3310 Harrison Street
Topeka, KS 66611
(913) 266-7013

National Wood Window and Door Association
1400 East Touhy Avenue
Des Plaines, IL 60018
(312) 299-5200

Small Homes Council-Building Research Council
University of Illinois
One East Saint Mary's Road
Champaign, IL 61820
(217) 333-1801

Steel Window Institute
1230 Keith Building
Cleveland, OH 44115
(216) 241-7333

Architectural Woodwork Institute (AWI)
South Walter Reed Drive
Arlington, VA 22206
(703) 671-9100

# FURTHER READING

The Historic Preservation Education Foundation sponsored an intensive, three-day conference in December 1986 on the repair, rehabilitation, and replacement of historic windows. *The Window Workbook for Historic Buildings* is a compendium of information that incorporates many of the papers presented at the conference as well as reprints of historic and current materials. Much of the material is out of print and not readily available elsewhere. Inquiries about the workbook should be addressed to the Historic Preservation Education Foundation, P.O. Box 27080, Central Station, Washington, D.C. 20037-7080. Articles and reprints in the workbook are listed below:

Brooks, Russell J. "Double Glazing in Wood Windows—The Muntin Problem."

Donaldson, Barry. "Special Considerations of Window Treatments for High-Rise Commercial Buildings."

Gutterman, Nan. "Windows in a Marine Environment: The Refurbishing/Replacement of the Windows at Ellis Island."

Kaplan, Marilyn E. "Windows, Historic Buildings, and the Requirements."

Love, Frederick R. "The Rehabilitation of Wooden Frames."

Moisson, James. "Protecting Interior Furnishings and Finishes from Sunlight Damage."

Park, Sharon C. " Steel Windows: Where We Are in 1986."

Pepperman, Alan J. "Repair/Replace With Wood Windows."

Sloan, Julie L. "Protecting Stained Glass."

Stivale, William. "Window Restoration—Evaluation and Planning."

———— . "In-House Restoration for Religious Institutions—An Alternative Approach."

Vieria, Robin K. "Energy Conservation Strategies for Windows in the Sunbelt."

Young, Graig W. "Aluminum Replacement Windows: Specifying to Assure Quality and Performance."

The *Old-House Journal*, a bimonthly magazine, provides practical advice for the professional as well as the do-it-yourselfer. Each issue features articles on specific rehabilitation problems with relevant sources of information and restoration products. A year's back issues are reprinted as the *Old-House Journal Yearbook*. In addition, the annual *Old-House Journal Catalog* lists more than a thousand companies that supply products and services for restoration. For ordering information contact the Old-House Journal Corporation, 69A Seventh Avenue, Brooklyn, NY 11217. Listed below are some of the articles on window repair that have appeared in the magazine over the past few years:

Clark, Susan. "Make Your Own Ornamental Wood Screens." (July 1981)

Cotton, J. Randall. "Return to Awnings." (July 1985)

Jones, Larry. "How to Install Weatherstripping." (April 1982)

———. "More About Double-Glazed Inserts." (September 1982)

Labine, Clem. "Rescuing Those 'Hopeless' Windows." (April 1982)

McConkey, James. "Rotten Window Sills." (January 1980)

"Movable Insulation." (April 1982)

O'Donnell, Bill. "Troubleshooting Old Windows." (January/February 1986)

Poore, Patricia. "Old Windows." (September 1980)

———. "Replacing Old Windows." (April 1982)

"Talk to Me of Windows." (April 1982)

"Weatherstripping." (September 1980)

In addition to the above-mentioned sources, consult the following publications for specific advice on a variety of problems facing anyone who is rehabilitating windows:

*Builders' Hardware*. Scranton, Pa.: International Textbook Company, 1908.

Byrne, Richard O. "Conservation of Historic Window Glass." *Association for Preservation Technology Bulletin,* vol. XIII, no. 3, 1981.

Carruthers, J. F. S. *The Weatherstripping of Windows and Doors*. Watford, England: Building Research Establishment, October 1981.

*A Comparison for Reducing Heat Loss Through Windows*. Berkeley, Calif.: U.S. Department of Energy, n.d.

"External Walls: Joints with Windows and Doors—Application of Sealants." Watford, England: Building Research Establishment, December 1985.

"External Walls: Joints with Windows and Doors—Detailing of Sealants." Watford, England: Building Research Establishment, December 1985.

Fisher, Charles. "Renewing Historic Windows." *Northeast Sun*, February 1985.

Halda, Bonnie J. "Specification Requirements for Proposed Window Replacement in Historic Buildings for Property Owners Seeking Federal Tax Benefits." Denver, Colo.: National Park Service, Rocky Mountain Regional Office, 1986.

————. "Specification Requirements for Proposed Storm Windows in Historic Buildings for Property Owners Seeking Federal Tax Benefits." Denver, Colo.: National Park Service, Rocky Mountain Regional Office, 1986.

Kidder, F. E. *Building Construction and Superintendence*. 4th ed. New York: William T. Comstock, 1902.

Konzo, Seichi. "Saving by Insulating Doors and Windows." *Council Notes,* vol. 4, no. 3, Winter 1980.

Leeke, John. "Making Window Sash." *Fine Homebuilding,* December 1983/January 1984.

Meyers, John H. *The Repair of Historic Wooden Windows*. Preservation Brief No. 9. Washington, D.C.: National Park Service, Preservation Assistance Division, 1981.

Nelson, Lee H., ed. *Interpreting the Secretary of the Interior's Standards for Rehabilitation*. Washington, D.C.: National Park Service, Preservation Assistance Division, n.d.

Park, Sharon C. *The Repair and Thermal Upgrading of Historic Steel Windows*. Preservation Brief No. 13. Washington, D.C.: National Park Service, Preservation Assistance Division, 1984.

"Preventing Decay in External Joinery." *Building Research Establishment Digest*, December 1985.

Stewart John D., et al. *The Schermerhorn Row Block: A Study in Nineteenth-Century Building Technology in New York City*. Waterford, N.Y.: New York State Office of Parks, Recreation and Historic Preservation, 1981.

Swiatosz, Susan. "A Technical History of Late Nineteenth-Century Windows in the United States." *Association for Preservation Technology Bulletin,* vol. XVII, no. 1, 1985.

Vonier, Thomas. "Next Window, Please." *Progressive Architecture,* August 1984.

# INDEX

air infiltration, *81*, 81–84, *82*, 113. *See also* weatherstripping

alligatoring, 75, *75*, 98–99

Aluminum Association (AA), 134

aluminum windows, 47

    caulking, 102

    conduction, 86

    replacement windows, *137*, 140–41, *147*, 147–50, *149*

    storm windows, 121

    water penetration and weathering, 68, 69

American Architectural Manufacturers Association (AAMA), 134, 135

*American Builder's Companion, The* (Benjamin), 23

*American House Carpenter, The* (Hatfield), 28

American National Standards Institute, 134

American Society for Testing and Materials (ASTM), 134

Architectural Aluminum Manufacturing Association, 134

*Architecture of Country Houses, The* (Downing), 28–29

austral-balance windows, 40, *41*

awning windows, 63

awnings, 126, 130, *131*


Badger, Daniel, 18

bay windows, 28

Beckett, H. E., 86

Benjamin, Asher, 23

blind stop, 54

blinds, *33*, 33–35, *34*, 130–31

    grades, 32

    venetian, *33*, 35, 130

bow windows, 38

brick mold, 53

*Brickbuilder, The*, 38

broad glass, 16
bronze windows, 39

casement sash, 25, 29, 36, 53–54, *54*
    operation, *77*
    simulated casement, *28*
    steel windows, 54, *55*
    wood windows, 25, 53–54, *54*
caulking, 83, 101–04, *102, 103*
channel balances, 58, *58*
check rail sash, 23, 41
Chicago windows, 41, 43, *43*
Colonial Revival windows, 36, *36*, 38, 40, 41
commercial buildings, 42–44
"common rising" sash, 29
condensation, 70–73, *71, 72*, 126
conduction, 84–87
    secondary sash glazing and, 126
copper windows, 43
    water penetration and weathering, 68, 69, *69*
*Cottage Residences* (Downing), 29
cottage-front windows, 28–29, 36, *37*, 41
crack perimeter, *65*, 83
crown glass, *16*, 16–17
Curtis windows, 41
cylinder glass, 16, *16*, 17, 19

doors, grades of, 32
dormer windows, *27*, 36, *37*
Downing, Andrew Jackson, 28–29
drawn glass process, 20
Dutch windows, *24*, 25

energy performance, 80–90
    air infiltration, *81*, 81–84, *82*, 113
    conduction, 84–87, 126
    radiation, 87–89, *88*
    *See also* weatherstripping
eyebrow dormer windows, 36, *37*
eyelid dormer windows, 36, *37*

Federal-style windows, 26, *26*, 27, *27*
Fenestra windows, 41, 46
fireglass, 19
fireproof windows, 42–43
    kalomein windows, 39
float glass, 20
French windows, 28, 53

gable sash, 36
Georgian Revival windows, 36, 40
Georgian-style windows, 17, 26
glazing, 53
    colored glass, 18
    compounds, 101–02, 104–05
    crown glass, 16–17
    cylinder glass, 16, *16*, 17, 19
    drawn glass process, 20
    fixed-frame glazing, 123
    float glass, 20
    insulating glass, 126–27
    leaded glass, 18
    manufacturing, 15–20, 29, 31
    plastic glass, 123–24
    plate glass, *18*, 18–19, 20, 31
    reinstalling old glass, 109
    repair, 109
    replacement glass, 109, 138, *141*
    rolled or rightcast glass, 20
    secondary sash, 125–27, *127*
    sheet glass, 16
    sidewalk lights, *18*, 19
    sizes, 40, 41
    stained glass, 18
    storm windows, 123–24
    wire glass, 19–20, *20*
Godfrey, A., 86
Gothic Revival windows, 28, 29, *30*, 60
Greek Revival windows, 26, 27, *27*, 28, *62*, *153*

hardware, *38*, 53, 54, *55*, 58, 110
Hatfield, R. G., 28

historic buildings. *See* landmark buildings

hopper windows, 63

Interior, Secretary of, Standards for Rehabilitation, 91, 95, 157, 158–59, 161–64

Italianate Revival windows, 28, 29, *31*, 42

joinery, 20–23, *22*
    replacement windows, 140

kalomein windows, 39

Lalique, René, 159

landmark buildings, 91, 153–60
    designation as, 154–59
    determining significance of, 159–60
    regulations and standards, 158–60
    rehabilitation guidelines, 161–64
    *See also* window rehabilitation

Landmarks Preservation Commission (New York City), 159

landscape windows, 41

Le Corbusier, 20

Lupton windows, 45, 46

Lupton's Sons Company, Philadelphia, 44

meeting stile, 54, *55*

metal windows, 38, 42–43
    air infiltration, *81*
    aluminum windows. *See* aluminum windows
    bronze windows, 39
    condensation, *72*, 73, *141*
    conduction, *85*, 85–86, *141*
    deterioration, *80*
    joinery, 140
    kalomein windows, 39
    paint failure, 76
    radiation, *88*
    replacement windows, 140–41
    steel windows. *See* steel windows
    water penetration and weathering, 68–69, *69*

metal working, 24

moldings, 35
    Colonial Revival windows, 36, 38
    "dripstone cap," *30*
    replacement windows, *148*, 148–49
Monckton, James H., 31
mullions, 53, 54
muntins, 49, 53, *138*

Nantucket, Mass., Jethro Coffin House, *25*
National Association of Architectural Metal Manufacturers
        (NAAMM), 134
*National Carpenter and Joiner, The* (Monckton), 31
National Park Service, Secretary of the Interior's Standards for
        Rehabilitation, 91, 95, 157, 158–59, 161–64
National Register of Historic Places, 155, 156, 157, 161
National Woodwork Manufacturers Association (NWMA), 134
New York City
    Bohemian Hall, 60, *61*
    Coty Building, *159*
    Morris-Jumel Mansion, *49*
    Schermerhorn Row, 21–22
New York City Landmarks Preservation Commission, 159
Newport, R.I., John Bannister House, *57*
noise infiltration, 90, 113

Ondoyant Glass, 20

paint
    failure, *67*, 73–76, *74*, *75*
    removal, 98–101, *99*
    repainting, 100–01
Palladian windows, 38
pantry windows, 35, *35*
parting bead, 54
parting stop, 54
parting strip, 54
pattern books, 31, 33
Pittsburgh Hardwood Door Company, 20
plastic glass, 123–24
plate glass, *18*, 18–19, 20, 31

Queen Anne windows, *35*, 35–36,
quilts, *129*

radiation, 87–89, *88*
rehabilitation of windows. *See* window rehabilitation
replacement windows, 133–51
    aluminum, *137*, 140–41, 147–50, *147*, *149*
    color, 139
    construction, 139–41
    design, 134
    dimensions and proportions, 136, 138
    durability, 144
    extent of replacement, 142–43
    field testing, 143
    finish, 139
    glass. *See* glazing
    installation, 142–43, *143*
    maintenance and repairs, 144–45
    operation of original window, 135
    options, 145–51
    performance standards, 134–35, 143
    product testing, 142
    quality control, 143
    shape, 136
    steel, 140–41, 146–47
    trim, 139
    unit replacement, *136*, 142
    vinyl, 150–51
    wood, 140, 145–46
residential buildings, 24–41
retrofit measures, 113–31. *See also specific headings, e.g.,*
    weatherstripping
Richmondtown, N.Y., Voorlezer's House, *54*

sash, 51–52, 53
    arched, *27*, *30*, *62*, *68*, *155*
    awning, 63
    casement, 25, 28, *28*, 29, 36, 53–54, *54*, *55*, 77
    check rail, 23, 41
    combination, 53, 63
    "common rising," 29

continuous, *46*, 46–47

counterbalanced, 42, 44

counterweighted sash, 42, 57, *57*

divided-light, 53

double-hung, *21*, *22*, 23, 25–28, 26, *27*, *28*, 29, 38, 40,
    42, 44, *50*, *52*, *54*, *56*, 56–58, 76–77, *154*

folding, 41

gable, 36

glass. *See* glazing

grades, 32

hopper, 63

meeting stiles, 54, *55*

multiple-light, 42

pivot, 38, *38*, *40*, 42, *43*, *44*, *47*, 53, 60, *60*, *61*, 63

projecting, 44, *45*

rail, 23, *23*

reversible, 38, *38*, 40

secondary sash glazing, 125–27, *127*

single-hung, 56, *56*

single-light, *51*

sliding, 25, 45, 53, 54, 60, *60*

spring-balance, 40, 42

stationary, *24*, 25, *26*, *27*, *36*, 53, *62*, 63

swinging, *24*, *41*, 42, 53, *54*

transom, 36

triple-hung, 25, 56, *57*

ventilating, *44*

vents, 54

vertical sliding, 25, *26*

*See also specific headings, e.g.,* cottage-front windows, steel windows

screens, 33, 126, 129–30

Second Empire Revival windows, 28, 29, 42

shades, 35, 89, 126, *129*, 129–30

Shaw, Edward, 27

sheet glass, 16

Shingle Style, 36

shutters, *54*, 89, 128–29

    metal, 42

    *See also* blinds

sidewalk lights, *18*, 19, *19*

sight line, 138

stained glass, 18

Standards for Rehabilitation, Secretary of the Interior's, 91, 95, 157, 158–59, 161–64

state historic preservation officer (SHPO), 157, 158

steel windows, 38–39, *39*, 40, 42–43

    casement sash, 54, *55*

    caulking, 102, *103*

    commercial buildings, 43–44, *44*, *45*, 47

    conduction, 86

    Fenestra windows, 41

    industrial buildings, 45, *46*, 47

    kalomein windows, 39

    paint removal, 100–01

    repair, 108–09, *108*, *111*

    replacement parts, 112–13

    replacement windows, 140–41, 146–47

    Vento windows, 41

    water penetration and weathering, 68

    weatherproofing, 38

Steel Windows Institute (SWI), 134

storm windows, 120–24, *121*, *124*, *125*

    condensation, 70

    exterior, 120–22, *122*

    interior, 122–24, *123*, 126, *126*

    wood, 53


tape balances, 58, *58*

Tarrytown, N.Y., Lyndhurst, 50

tenement buildings, 38

Thermopane, 126

transom sash, 36

tube balances, 58, *59*

Tudor windows, 40

Twindow, 126

Twinpane, 126


vault lights, *18*, 19, *19*

venetian blinds, *33*, 35, 130

ventilating sash, 44

Vento windows, 41

vents, 54

vinyl windows, 150–51

water penetration, 64–69, *67, 68, 69. See also* weatherstripping
water spray rack, 70, *70*
weatherstripping
    replacement windows, 144
    retrofit measures, 113–19, *114, 115, 116, 117, 118, 119, 120*
    *See also* water penetration
Wholesale Sash, Door, and Blind Manufacturers Association, 33
    official grades of sash, doors, blinds, 32
window rehabilitation
    analysis of conditions, 77–90
    budget, 92
    caulking, 83, 101–04, *102, 103*
    cleaning, 98
    evaluation of conditions and problems, 49–95
    extent and sequence of, 91
    glass. *See* glazing
    goals, 51
    hardware, 110
    landmark buildings, 153–60
    maintenance, 97–113
    new components, 93–94
    occupancy of building and, 91–92
    paint removal, 98–101, *99*
    physical problems, 63
    repainting, 100–01
    repair of existing windows, 93, 105–13, *106, 107, 108, 111*
    replacement of window components, 93–94
    replacement of window units, 94–95
    replacement parts, 110–13
    replacement windows. *See* replacement windows
    retrofit measures, 113–31
    Standards for Rehabilitation, 91, 95, 157, 158–59, 161–64
    strategies, 92–95
    survey, 78
    weatherstripping. *See* weatherstripping
windows
    air infiltration, *81*, 81–84, *82*, 113
    blind stop, 54
    brick mold, 53

casing, 52–53

caulking, 83, 101–04, *102, 103*

cleaning, 38, 40, 43, 98

commercial and public buildings, 42–44

condensation, 70–73, *71, 72*, 126

conduction, 84–87, 126

construction techniques, 15–24

crack perimeter, *65*, 83

curved, 38, *38*

deterioration, 63–76, *79, 80*

energy performance. *See* energy performance

fireproof, 42–43

frame, 52–53

glass. *See* glazing

hardware, *38*, 52, 53, 54, *55*, 58, 100

heads, 52

historical overview, 15–47

industrial buildings, 44–47

interior stops, 54

jambs, 52, 53

landscape windows, 41

noise infiltration, 90, 113

operation, 76–77

paint. *See* paint

parting stops, 54

parts, 51–53, *52, 53*

radiation, 87–89, *88*

replacement windows. *See* replacement windows

residential buildings, 24–41

sash. *See* sash

sight line, 138

sills, 52

stools, 54

stops, 52, 54

tenement buildings, 38

trim, 35, 38

types of, 53–63

visual inspection, 78–80

water penetration, 64–69, *67, 68, 69*

*See also specific types of windows, e.g.:* bay windows;
     cottage–front windows

*Windows: Performance, Design and Installation* (Beckett and
        Godfrey), 86
wire glass, 19–20, *20*
wood windows, 20–23, *22*, 41
    air infiltration, *81*, *82*, 84
    casement sash, *25*, 53–54, *54*
    caulking, 102, *102*
    condensation, *72*, 73
    conduction, *85*, 86
    fillers and consolidants, 105, 107
    joinery, 140
    kalomein windows, 39
    paint failure, 76
    paint removal, 98–100
    radiation, *88*
    repair, 105–07, *106*
    replacement parts, 110–12
    replacement windows, 140, 145–46
    water penetration and weathering, 38, 66–68